SOME PEOPLE ARE DEAD

PART ESSAY, PART MEMOIR, PARTS UNKNOWN

JAMES SCOTT BELL

COMPENDIUM PRESS

ISBN 10: 0-910355-41-X

ISBN 13: 978-0-910355-41-4

CONTENTS

INTRODUCTION

"Don't fear the reaper." - Blue Oyster Cult

"I'm not afraid of death. I just don't want to be there when it happens." - Woody Allen

"Everybody has got to die, but I have always believed an exception would be made in my case. Now what?" - Last words of William Saroyan

William Saroyan
(1908 - 1981)

Many years ago William Saroyan came out with one of the strangest books I've ever read, *Obituaries*. I bought it in hardcover, first edition, because I was a Saroyan fan. (For those of you who don't know the name Saroyan, know this: he was one of America's most famous writers in the 1930s and into the 1940s, and though his literary reputation has suffered since his death in 1981, he deserves his spot at the table of American letters, and if you want to read one of the best collections of short stories ever, then go get a copy of *My Name is Aram*.)

Why do I say it was such a strange book? Because there is not a single indent or paragraph break in the entire thing. It is divided into numbered chapters, but each chapter is just one long block of text, Saroyan's mind riffing, and the chapters end only when

Saroyan has decided he has nothing more to say on whatever he's talking about.

And what is it he is talking about? Death, yes. But also life and sons and lovers and writing and anything else that mattered to him. And a lot mattered to him.

His method was this: he had a January, 1977 edition of *Variety*, Hollywood's "bible" in those days, and went through the list of names of those in the movie industry who had, in the previous year, passed on to that big projection room in the sky. Some of the names he knew, having been around Hollywood a bit. But most names he did not know, yet that didn't stop him from using a decedent as a launching pad, and going off on whatever tangent was triggered in Saroyan's fertile mental soil.

Here's an example:

> Joe Bigelow. He died, too. And I never knew him, I am sorry to say, for I like the name. It is a rollicking name, O, O, Bigelow. I hope he had a good life and a very good death, for of course it would be absurd not to know that there are as many kinds of death as there are kinds of life, pieces of action and experience, or marbles. If you remember when marbles had a meaning in your life, you have surely not forgotten that there were all kinds of them, and even if you paid Woolworth's a dime for a little sack of marbles, when you brought the marbles out of hiding into visibility, they invariably seem to be priceless treasures.

From Joe Bigelow, to life and death, and then to marbles. After that passage Saroyan moves, somehow, through the unique wiring of his brain—and that, after all, is what makes a good writer, a real writer: he or she can somehow put that wiring on a page and make people care—to the streets of Calcutta, and the women on the street, and from there to China and Russia, and all the time meditating on life and death. And then the chapter ends.

The whole book is like that! You read it thinking, with each chapter, he can't really carry this off, can he? For a whole book? But he did, and the critics, who were not always kind to him, responded favorably.

Here's what Publishers Weekly said about *Obituaries:*

> *Obituaries* turns out to be an astonishing book, a profound and even original meditation about death and our only possible answer to it: the way we live. It is also about sex, being a parent, Saroyan's Armenian memories, talks with Dickens's ghosts, Hollywood riffraff, and anything else this wise raconteur, in his inimitable way, deems worthy. *Obituaries* is solemn, beautiful, hilarious, raunchy, a heart-breakingly sad and funny testament and one of Saroyan's finest books.

It was all of those things but, sadly, as I checked on Amazon today, I found it was not available in digital format. Only used copies priced from $0.01 for paperback and $0.02 for hardback, which is about as illustrative of the fleetingness of glory as there is. Some new copies fetched a higher price, which I think is only fair to a writer like Saroyan, who loved to write for the sheer joy of it and, I think, to stave off his own death, which he knew would come but did not know quite how to deal with. So he dealt with it in *Obituaries,* which was very nearly his last book.

So why have I decided to write a book like that?

First, at the beginning of the year 2015, I decided to up my writing production. As history moves along I know I only have so much time on this orb, and I'm a writer, so I want to do as much of it as I can before I leave.

Second, I've always liked it that Saroyan was not just a novelist and short story writer and playwright, but also a roving and robust essayist, observer, and memoirist. I don't know that anyone would be interested in a whole JSB memoir, outside of my own family (and maybe not even all of them!). But perhaps some short trips down Memory Lane would not tax the weary too much. Plus, the essays and thoughts and musings of authors have always interested me. Ray Bradbury was another fiction writer who loved to speculate via the essay form, so I'm following the pattern of two of my writing heroes in this book.

Third, writing this way, in the morning, after looking at some of the obits of 2015, and just letting go, well, it's simply good writing practice—to stretch your mind and expand your style—and as far as I know only Saroyan had done a book like this before, that is, taking as his daily writing prompt an actual obituary, letting his mind go wherever it wanted to go, and making the ride as entertaining as possible. I give him full credit for this idea and wanted to join him.

Fourth, there are things you learn about life that at some point you think somebody else might find valuable, or at least interesting, which is the true art of the essayist, after all, and I love a good essay, like old Montaigne who started the genre, and Joseph Epstein, who can make anything, even a pant leg, seem important, or William Zinsser, whose essays and little books are smooth as honey and hilarious, much like Mark Twain, who could also write, and Saroyan himself, peppering his musings with his philosophy of life, which was not something systematic but vibrant, alive, changing, curious—that's what I want to write, too.

Finally, it was only a small publisher that took a chance on Saroyan's book, and I don't know that it would have been published today, which is a shame, but here we are in the new world of self-publishing and this is exactly the kind of book that needs self-publishing, the way Walt Whitman needed self-publishing, and there I go, putting my name up alongside William Saroyan, Ray Bradbury, and Walt Whitman, not to mention Mark Twain. That's called cheeky, or chutzpah, or maybe even hubris, but let me state that I look at those men as standards, not equals, and entertain the notion that perhaps, had they seen my modest effort here, they might have nodded with something like approval, and I think they would have because they would have understood my motives. They all loved writing, needed it, and never stopped until their bodies ran out and they were summoned to the offices of the Great Editor for a final review.

· · ·

Had I been able, I would have simply stated, "I will do my best, gents, like you all did, and I won't ever stop, and by the way, thanks for all the words."

SOME PEOPLE ARE DEAD

Anita Ekberg died. She was 83.

She was blonde and she was beautiful, she was foreign and she spoke English. That could make you a big sex symbol back in the 1960s. Brigitte Bardot was another like that. Britt Ekland and May Britt—who I could never tell apart, except that one of them was married to Sammy Davis, Jr. at one time—they were like that, too.

Sammy Davis, Jr., by the way, died years ago, but had to be one of the most talented performers we've ever produced in this country, and truly under appreciated. Singer, dancer, dramatic and comedic actor, stand-up comic. Sammy was so good he managed to move past the more extreme forms of racial prejudice at work in those days, the Eisenhower days and the Kennedy days. He hung out with the Rat Pack, which was founded by Mr. Frank Sinatra, and which was not the healthiest pack to hang with, that

Las Vegas late-night crowd, that drinking and smoking and (what was called) "carrying on" gang. But that's how many a man measured his manliness back then, and another way was the kind of gal you had on your arm, and Sammy hit the American male lottery when he married one of the Swedish sex kittens, as they were called, with Britt in the name, and it was May Britt (I've taken the time to look it up, but kept the above recollection because when you were a kid back then and not paying attention it really did get all confused in your mind).

The marriage to May Britt did not last, which reminded me of another marriage between an American celebrity and a Swedish blonde that did not last. This American celebrity was a star professional golfer, maybe the best golfer who ever played the game, up until the year 2009 when it came out that this golfer was "carrying on" with all manner of womanhood off the course and on the road, managing to keep it hush-hush until it wasn't, until some of the women started to talk, and until it could not be denied anymore, and until one fateful night when his Swedish-born wife discovered undeniable evidence of her husband's adulterous amours and woke him up and scratched his face and chased him with a golf club—oh, irony!—outside, where the golfer jumped into an Escalade and tried to drive away, but instead drove right into some hedges and then a tree—which was another irony, as it turned out, because after this the golfer was never the same, and his golf drives often went into hedges and trees.

But I digress.

.   .   .

Anita Ekberg became a sensation starring in a Federico Fellini film called *La Dolce Vita*, mainly because of a scene in the Trevi Fountain in Rome. I have never been to Rome, even though all roads are supposed to lead there. That's not true, I can tell you that with complete confidence. There is no road that goes from Los Angeles to Rome. But I will get there someday to look upon the ruins, to note that the greatest empire the world has ever known was not able to sustain itself, that it is a law of history that civilizations perish, for various reasons, maybe the chief one being that they rot from the inside, the moral side, the virtue side, and I guess that's what Will Durant said about it. Durant the great popularizer of history, said that civilizations begin stoic and end epicurean. You have to be stoic to be tough and fight and have a revolution and keep a country going, even through civil wars; then you get to the place where you seem to be in control and what happens? The people become lazy and pleasure-seeking, and it's-all-about-me, and before you know it you don't have that civilization anymore.

So maybe I'll go to Rome to have a look at those ruins, and remind myself that no country is immune from the lessons of history (the #1 lesson being that we are dunderheads who refuse to learn the lessons of history). And that means this country, too, where they don't teach the real lessons of history in school anymore, and try surviving that, Jack.

The glory of sex-kitten stardom is also fleeting, and Anita Ekberg had plastic surgery to try to keep it for a while longer and then said she regretted that decision, that she wished she had "grown old gracefully," which is the very best thing any of us can do as the finish line of life comes into view.

~

Around the same time Anita Ekberg shuffled off her mortal coil, a man named **Bert A. Cramer** died.

His death was the opposite of Anita Ekberg's. Bert A. Cramer was never in a Federico Fellini film and as far as I know never stepped into the Trevi Fountain. I say *as far as I know* because I can only go so far as the obituary in *The Missoulian,* which is the newspaper of the town of Missoula, Montana. I found this obit by asking Google News to deliver me some obituaries on the same date that Ekberg's appeared, and got this hit to Mr. Bert A. Cramer, whose notice came out exactly like this:

Bert A. Cramer 89, died at his home Saturday, Jan. 10. Arrange-ments are pending with Cremation and Burial Society of the Rockies.

That's it, that's all, and there is the final notice of a man's life, and what kind of life was it? We don't know. Was Bert a happy man? Did he have family? There is no mention of family, or friends asking folks to send donations to a charity or flowers to a home.

Did Bert A. Cramer die alone? There is nothing much sadder than that.

.   .   .

Or was Bert A. Cramer a beloved member of the community, only there wasn't enough space to give him a real send off? Or no one wanted to spend the money on a bigger notice?

How did Bert A. Cramer play this game of life before he cashed in his chips?

I suppose the guy who thought up that metaphor (chips, cashed) thought life itself was a gamble. It's more like a game you can play skillfully or like a doofus. Don't be a doofus. That would be an appropriate headstone for most men: *Beloved husband and father. And he wasn't a doofus.*

Luise Rainer died. She was 104.

She was a terrific actress, and the first film performer to win back-to-back Oscars. She took home the top prize for her performance as Anna Held in *The Great Ziegfeld*. Then the next year as O-Lan in *The Good Earth*. She was at the top of the heap, as they say, in the 1930s—a pixie-ish beauty, a superb thespian. But she wouldn't take any crap from Louis B. Mayer, head of MGM, and in those days you either took his crap or you got booted out of the studio and perhaps shunned by the rest of Hollywood. Louis the Lousy made good on his threats and drummed Luise the Luminous out of the business.

.   .   .

Nobody's going to rediscover Mayer. But new generations will catch Rainer's movies and see what she was. And isn't that all we can ask of life—that we be remembered well? That we'll leave behind something of substance, and the courage of our convictions?

Luise Rainer was interviewed on TCM when she was 100. When she spoke about her approach to acting, "from the inside, out," her eyes were keen and intelligent. She talked about getting into the character of O-Lan, and all of a sudden her face changed and it was seventy-three years ago, and she *was* O-Lan. It was magical, that moment, the kind of moment Luise Rainer gave us in her all-too-short career.

Louis the Lousy has died, and is unheralded. Luise has died, and the angels are getting some lessons in acting, so the next time they appear to shepherds they can do a little Shakespeare along with their singing.

There are vile people in this world and they have another world to go to, even if they don't believe they do and even if they never think about it. Not to believe it merely makes one ignorant. Never to think about it makes one a fool.

On this good Earth, we can only do our best, do our work, honor our craft, whatever that is, and trust that somewhere and sometime the scales will balance out.

～

Leonard C. Meeker died. He was 98, a good old age, if one is still alert, like Luise Rainer was.

All I know about Mr. Meeker is what I read in the *Washington Post*, and it said he was a State Department legal officer who served as U.S. ambassador to Romania from 1969 to 1973. I suppose if you're going to be an ambassador, there are worse places you could be than Romania. The *Post* said he joined the State Department after World War II. But then came the money quote: "Mr. Meeker played a major role during the Cuban missile crisis of 1962 in developing a quarantine of Cuba instead of a blockade, which could have been considered an act of war."

I was too young to remember the actual Cuban missile crisis, but later learned it was about a couple of commies, Khrushchev and Castro, getting together to bring big honkin' missiles to Cuba, which you'll note is a mere 90 miles from Key West, Florida.

What I knew about Khrushchev and Castro I learned from *Mad* magazine. The '60s was the golden age of *Mad*, and they had great caricaturists and intelligent writers, and always did satires based on movies and musicals, and you'd have Castro, with his cigar, singing alongside the bald-headed Khrushchev. This, folks, is one way to teach your children well.

Al Martinez died. He was 85. Martinez was a great local writer, by which I mean the kind of writer who specializes in a place. Like Herb Caen in San Francisco, or Mike Royko in

Chicago, or Jimmy Breslin in New York. All those guys were first and foremost newspapermen, they took pride in that, which meant they took pride in their writing and worked hard to make it look effortless.

Martinez wrote about Los Angeles. He could mix in humor and pathos, make you laugh and cry at the same time. He wasn't sappy. He had just the right touch of grace, humor, and mercy mixed with a wise and sometimes snarky gimlet-eye.

Gimlet-eye, by the way, is a great term most people don't know today. A *gimlet* is an old-fashioned tool, looking sort of like a corkscrew, that is used to bore holes in wood. In other words, to go deeper. So if you have a gimlet-eye, you can *see* deeper, get below the surface, which is what a really great newspaper columnist does, and Martinez was a really great newspaper columnist.

I should mention that a gimlet is also the name of a drink, made with gin or vodka and some Rose's lime juice. The manly-man hunters in Hemingway stories drank gimlets while on safari. But too many of those kind of gimlets did not let you see deeper because you couldn't see much at all after you passed out. Which is what many newspapermen did, too, back in the day, hard-drinking scribes a lot of them were. Part of the reason, I think, is that it was what manly-men were supposed to do in that profession, so they did it, they kept bottles in their desk drawers or filing cabinets, and drank all the time, which is not good for your liver or your profession.

. . .

Martinez was also a great writer of outrage, when such was deserved. He had a famous column in 1986 about how a local community had driven an interracial couple out of their neighborhood. The column began, *Hate won last weekend in Westchester.*

Take a look at that sentence. Did you notice that it's not: *Hate won in Westchester last weekend.*

The first is sonorous. The second is a clunker. That's part of what made Martinez so good, and it's true for all the great writers over time, especially the kind that used to write for newspapers: the ability to avoid the clunky sentence. Writers of all types need to attend to their sentences, because strings of them are what make a story and you want pearls on that string, not bits of moldy clay.

Toward the end Martinez glimpsed wistfully at himself and his advancing age. One of his last columns on the L.A. Observed website began like this:

> When old men get together over poker and a few beers they no longer talk only about babes and politics. They also talk about their bladders and their prostate glands.
>
> On this night they hit three out of four. No politics.

In another column, titled "Always Leave Them Laughing," he reflects on having to be hooked up to oxygen for the rest of his days:

Now I walk along with tubes up my nose, carrying a small canister of O2, the result of having COPD, knowing my own days are limited, but grateful for the freedom the tube and the tank have provided. When I do stop for a drink, I slam the tank on the bar and holler, "Fill 'er up, Jimmy!"

Everyone laughs.

That was what he always wanted to do with a column. Leave them laughing. Or crying. Or thinking. He refused to leave anyone bored.

And speaking of leaving them laughing, **Taylor Negron** died. He was only 57. He was a standup comedian and actor in Los Angeles. You may remember him as the pizza delivery guy who interrupts a class at Ridgemont High, bringing a pie to the stoner played by Sean Penn. Negron did a lot of roles like that.

Early in his career I saw him perform at the Improv in Los Angeles. He was part of a team doing real improvisation, where the audience calls out something and the actors immediately go into a scene. When I was an actor, doing improv was my favorite thing. In high school I was on an award-winning team. Later on in New York, the improv thing worked for me when I was doing my first professional role Off-Broadway in a production of *Othello*.

This was at the Roundabout Theatre when it was on West 23d Street. I had just moved to New York from L.A., wanting to be an actor, wanting to be like Brando, and you had to go to New York to be like Brando, you had to start out on the stage. I'd managed to get a room at a Catholic rooming house right across the street from the Roundabout. The Leo House it was called, run by an order of nuns who did not brook any nonsense, boy, and who gave me a room that was the size of a jail cell, and had one bed, one desk, one lamp, and a crucifix on the wall. And for 15¢ in the morning they'd give me a hard-boiled egg. This assuaged my Protestant appetite for about ten minutes. I was living the life, I was.

One day I walked over to the Roundabout and went in and told them I was an actor and that I'd volunteer to do any work to get a shot at auditioning. They happily hired me on the spot, and paid me something like five bucks a night (it was probably more, but it felt like five bucks a night), to push scenery around, prepare props and all that backstage stuff. I worked as a temp typist during the day, and pushed scenery at night, and was happy to do it all because I was a young, struggling actor and thought there was poetry in that.

Then came the time for the Roundabout's next production, which was *Othello,* and they'd already decided to cast me. Yes! Me! In a non-speaking role, and which included extra duty moving scenery and preparing props. For a slight raise in pay, so slight that I could only get one extra egg each day from the nuns.

But I was ecstatic! I was in a real, honest-to-goodness New York stage production. Not only that. It was Shakespeare!

.   .   .

Our Othello was the marvelous actor Earle Hyman, better known to most of you as Bill Cosby's father on *The Cosby Show*. In point of fact Earle is one of the great Othellos. He is also a very nice man. And happily, at the time of this writing, he is still with us.

Once, we were chatting backstage and I told him that someday I would love to play Iago. Earle said I would be perfect for it because I had such an open, honest face (this was before I went to law school). That, after all, is what makes Iago powerful. Othello calls him, "My friend ... honest, honest Iago." And if the part is played right there is even a touch of sympathy for Iago at the end as he's dragged off to be tortured to death.

Well, as the rehearsals went on I began, just for fun, to trot out my improvisational skills, and started doing voice impressions of the various actors. When I was in junior high school I used to love impressionists, like Frank Gorshin, who appeared a lot on the Ed Sullivan show. I started doing voices at school and amused my teachers. Some, anyway. Not Mrs. Flores, who was about 98 years old and did not find junior high school boys to be amusing in any way, shape, form, or function. She was probably right about this.

So I was doing voice impressions of the cast of Othello, and everyone loved it and cracked up when I did them. The show went on, I happily walked out onstage a couple of times in my tights and tunic, said nothing, then happily walked off and pushed scenery and prepared props.

· · ·

Then one night a classic theatre trope took place. You know the one. It's where the star of the show breaks an ankle and a chorus girl is put on in her place, and becomes a star! This, of course, was the basic plot of one of my favorite movies, *All About Eve,* wherein Eve Harrington, a star-struck kid, latches onto Margo Channing, a true diva and theater legend (played by Bette Davis, and based in part on Tallulah Bankhead), and deviously plots to waylay Margo from a performance for which Eve is the under-study. Eve invites all the big critics to the performance and becomes a star! At the aging Margo's expense.

So one night in New York there was a subway outage and the people in Brooklyn couldn't get over to the city. One of those people was the actor who played Montano in our *Othello.* Montano is not a large role, but it *is* a speaking role. And we had no understudy.

Someone in the cast suggested to the frantic stage manager that I could do it, since I knew all the lines and imitated the actor. Huzzah! They put me in the role! The stage manager walked me through the blocking—where I was supposed to stand and walk during my scene—and I was ready to become a star!

I walked into the dressing room to get into costume. The whole cast was there, including our Iago, who was applying his makeup and who had a wonderful, deep voice that could drip with droll dismissiveness if he so desired. And as I entered, loud enough for everyone to hear, he said, "Well, well. If it isn't Eve Harrington!"

· · ·

Everybody laughed. It was a perfect line and a perfect delivery. And I was perfect in the role that night, I will tell you without false humility, though the next night I went back to being a mute walk-on and did not rocket to stardom. The real world is unjust.

So I appreciate good improvisational work, and Taylor Negron, I vividly recall, was superb, the best of the team that night at the Improv. I remembered his name after that, and was ever after pleased to see him show up in something, like an episode of *Seinfeld*. He was always funny.

And that's not a bad legacy, is it, to be funny and entertaining and leave people with good feelings? It's what a writer like me wants to do with his books, leave a good feeling behind and do that as much as possible. A good feeling doesn't have to be happy, either. It can mean that you've given a reader an emotional experience and when they finish they think, like a kid on a roller coaster, they want to do that again.

Taylor Negron made people want to see him again, even though most people did not know his name.

Good work, Taylor.

And as long as we're speaking of Shakespeare, I moved back to Hollywood after my triumph in *Othello* and was cast in a production of *Hamlet* at a little theatre in Hollywood, in the crucial role of Rosencrantz. In fact, I received the greatest notice of my acting career in that production. Very rarely do critics mention the actor playing either Rosencrantz or Guildenstern in a review of Shakespeare's classic. But a Hollywood trade paper said that James Scott Bell was "nicely oily" as Rosencrantz. What a great critic that was! Oily was exactly what I was going for!

Also in that production, as Laertes, was a young actor who was, for lack of a better word, intense. He was not nicely oily, he was lightning in tights. He kept to himself mostly, but one day we were backstage waiting around for the cast to be called, and I asked him what he was into, and he said making it as an actor. He also said he was living with his brother and not bringing in very much dough at the moment, but was hoping things would change soon. He was, in short, a fellow thespian knowing that the odds were long against massive success, but going for it because that's what he wanted to do.

His name was Ed Harris. In fact, it still is.

It was a few years later that I was walking past a drug store and saw a display of a magazine, I think it was *Newsweek*, and Ed Harris was on the cover. He had on an astronaut suit. He was playing the role of John Glenn in the big new movie *The Right Stuff*. He hasn't stopped working since.

My acting career, such as it was, hit its heights with some commercial work. You may have seen me push a tray of hamburgers at McDonald's, pour some Pepsi at a picnic, or play football with the guys at the beach before breaking out some suds. Or not. But I will say they paid me some nice royalties all the way through law school. So my acting did eventually pay a few ducats.

As Iago once said, "Put money in thy purse!"

Ray Bradbury's home died. It was 84 years old.

For years the great Bradbury lived in this house. He and his wife raised four daughters there, and there he lived when he wrote so many classics, like *The Illustrated Man* and *Dandelion Wine*.

I got to meet Ray Bradbury on a few occasions because he was very much an L.A. writer and loved his city, especially its libraries, and one night he came out to the re-opening of the Woodland Hills branch, which was my branch as a kid, and the city had done a remodel and closed the site for about a year. At the grand re-opening I snuck to the front of the crowd. I wanted to be the first one to check out a book at the new library, because it was *my* library, you see, and I deserved it. And out of the corner of my eye I saw another fellow who seemed, like Cassius, to have that lean and hungry look, and I remembered what Shakespeare said about such men: they are dangerous. This man seemed to know what I was thinking, and I knew what he was thinking, and when the doors of the new library opened, we both walked quickly, side by side like two Olympic walkers striding, and I went right up to the checkout desk and grabbed a paperback on a rack as I did, and laid it down and pulled out my card, and the librarian issued me the first book ever checked out in the new building.

I looked behind me and saw the other guy with a book in his hand and a rueful smile. Nice try, sir, and thanks for playing, but this is *my* library.

Somewhere in my home is the receipt for the book I checked out. I can't remember what it was now, because it didn't matter. I hope it wasn't erotica.

So Ray Bradbury came to speak one night at the new Woodland Hills branch, and he had a walker by then, but he spoke lovingly of books and writing and doing the script for *Moby-Dick,* and other things. Then he sat and signed books and I had my copy of *Zen in the Art of Writing* with me, and as he signed it he asked if I was a writer and I said, Yes. And he asked me what my schedule was, and I said I wrote five days a week and took off weekends for my family, and his eyes brightened and he said, "That's the way to do it!" He said that because that's how he, Ray Bradbury, had run his life when his children were young.

Here's what the house looked like when Bradbury lived there:

This is how the gutted remains looked just before final teardown:

You know what this is a metaphor of? The ultimate truth that commerce chews up art, for better or worse. Listed for $1,495,000, the house sold for $1,765,000, and then got torn down.

.   .   .

It's also a picture of what I said in the introduction to this book, about William Saroyan's own volume, *Obituaries*: All glory is fleeting.

Which in Latin is *Sic transit gloria mundi*.

Which applies to all of us, even Napoleon. He is better associated with a pastry now. What school kids know that he conquered a large swath of the world a long time ago? Or that he put his hand inside his coat? Or had a little curl over his forehead? Or tried to invade Russia?

Homes, like glory, also flee.

Raymond Chandler's old home in La Jolla, CA, where he wrote some of his classic tales, was bought and torn down. Same for Rudolph Valentino's Hollywood mansion, which was so fancy it had its own nickname, Falcon Lair. Because of the Valentino mystique, it remained pretty much as is until 2006, when the new owners bulldozed it.

By the way, Rudolph Valentino is buried in a crypt in the Hollywood Forever Cemetery, where my grandfather worked toward the end of his life, as a salesman. Arthur Scott Bell had been one of the top ten Encyclopedia Britannica salesmen during the Great Depression. He could spin a yarn like nobody's business, a natural storyteller, and I would visit him at the cemetery and go around and look at the graves of the famous actors, like Tyrone Power and Douglas Fairbanks.

And then to Valentino's crypt, which for years and years after his death got a visit from a mysterious woman in a black veil, who would come there every year.

Another famous Hollywood mansion had the nickname Pickfair. That was a combination of its owners, Mary Pickford and Douglas Fairbanks, who were the original glamour couple of Hollywood.

Pia Zadora, who is known to some as a singer, bought Pickfair (or, rather, her very rich and considerably older husband at the time, bought Pickfair) and she directed it to be torn down because there was a ghost in it. She said the ghost was of a woman who had died at Pickfair while having an affair with Douglas Fairbanks, which seems to me a serious accusation to level when the ghost of Doug is not around to rebut the charges.

Douglas Fairbanks and Mary Pickford got a divorce in 1936.

Pia Zadora and her rich husband got a divorce in 1993.

All things must end, either by divorce, or death, or getting torn down. This is the way of life, and we are wise to consider what sort of building we put on our foundations.

Bob Boyd died. He was 84.

Bob Boyd will go down as one of those people who landed in the right place at the wrong time. You couldn't get worse timing from a German comedian.

He was the basketball coach at the University of Southern California at the exact same time a man named John Wooden was the coach at the University of California, Los Angeles.

Bob Boyd was a great coach. John Wooden was a legend. Bob Boyd got some really good players. John Wooden got the best. In fact, the first year Bob Boyd coached at USC, their cross-town rival UCLA introduced a player who stood 7 feet 1 inch tall. His name was Lew Alcindor. He would later change his name to Kareem Abdul-Jabbar.

At one stretch John Wooden snagged seven National Championships *in a row*. That will never be done again, in any sport. Bob Boyd got to sit on a bench and watch it happen, year after year.

I was into basketball in those days. I was good, too. I went to the John Wooden basketball camp. I got to talk to the great man, and get coached by him and his assistants. I don't know if Bob Boyd had a basketball camp, but if he did he was probably just as frustrated getting campers when Wooden ran his program across town.

Here's the thing about life: while timing might not be everything, it's a pretty big thing, and unless you control time, like Tom Cruise in *Edge of Tomorrow*, you better get used to lousy timing and not let it bother you. You've got to get your Stoic on and not worry about the things you can't control. Don't even worry about the things you *can* control. Just don't worry. Work. Take action. Worry and frustration are for the birds, and I don't think birds worry, except maybe the small ones flying as fast as they can to get away from hawks.

And here's another thing Bob Boyd had to come to terms with: there's always going to be somebody, somewhere, who is better than you at something. I wanted to be a voice impressionist at one time in my life, but Rich Little was better at it. I wanted to be a great basketball player, and I was good for a guy who was 6'3" and slow. I was a great shooter, I could stack up with anybody on that score, except maybe Reggie Miller of UCLA who was probably the best pure shooter of all time (maybe until Steph Curry) and who was taller and faster than I. And that went for everything else I did, or you do.

But you can't let that stop you. Unless you want to quit, give up, take your ball and go home, you keep doing what you do, you keep trying and getting knocked down and getting back up and trying again. You do that until you die, and maybe in the afterlife you keep going, too.

. . .

I know that every year Bob Boyd gritted his teeth and said to himself, *This will be our year. This is it.* He kept believing, he had to or he'd fold like cheap lawn chair.

And that's the way Bob Boyd coached, and he got close. Oh yes, I remember one game where he had the great Paul Westphal on his team and they almost beat UCLA. I was at that game and I even stood outside the USC locker room because I'd written a letter to Paul Westphal and he was kind enough to write back and said he'd be glad to meet me, so I was there when he came out and man, the look on his face, dejection, because he had given his all, everything he had, had played a great game, and still came up short against the great UCLA, but he shook my hand anyway and that's how you handle disappointment. You feel bad for a time, but you don't let it sink you, you get up the next day and start again, fight again, and maybe that's all we can really ask out of life, the freedom to try again even after you get kicked in the mouth with a cosmic Wingtip.

Even when the timing is lousy.

Al Bendich, who died at the age of 85, got out of law school at just the right time, for him at least, because this was back in the late 1950s and there was a robust revolution going on in poetry and literature, called the Beat movement. I'm talking writers like Jack Kerouac and poets like Allen Ginsberg, and it was an intoxicating time because poetry and prose were breaking free of constraints, just like women and blacks were breaking free, and the whole Eisenhower apple cart was getting tipped, with apples rolling all over the place, and it was a revolution that had to happen, and there was a restlessness in writers who wanted to be free, and Allen Ginsberg was probably the most famous—or notorious, if you like your poetry to rhyme and be delicate and served with tea.

Ginsberg wrote a poem called *Howl*, and it was taken by many to be obscene, and the man who published the poem, another great poet named Lawrence Ferlinghetti, who owned City Lights Bookstore in San Francisco, was even charged with obscenity over *Howl* and was hauled into court, and there was Al Bendich, just two years out of Berkeley's Boalt Hall Law School, ready to defend the publisher of the poem on free speech grounds. I've read *Howl*, I own a copy, and it has obscene language in it, which is not for me, I can do without it, and I think the poem itself would have been better without it, but I am not the poet and that's not really the important thing here, because when it comes to speech I may be offended by what you say and what you write, but I don't want to toss you in the can for that, I want to offer my own speech, and I want both of us to be free.

So Ferlinghetti got charged, and on his defense team was Al Bendich, but the lead attorney was a famous San Francisco lawyer named Jake Erlich, who was a legend in his time, who would win jury trials right and left, even murder trials, and showed up in court dressed in the most expensive suits and jewelry—he wore cufflinks that cost, in those days, $25,000, and that's no joke, that's like $250,000 in today's money—and Erlich commanded the stage and made his case to the judge (it was a bench trial, which means only before a judge, not a jury) and was flamboyant and all. But it was the young Bendich, who wore suits he bought off the rack and buttoned his sleeves with the buttons provided with the shirts, who argued the United States Constitution, and that was the argument that convinced the judge to throw out the obscenity charge against Lawrence Ferlinghetti. And not only that, the judge who heard the case was a Sunday School teacher, named Horn, and his opinion was something of a landmark, holding that if a piece of writing had "redeeming social importance" then the objectionable parts did not take the work outside the protection of the First Amendment, and that was major for writers everywhere, and even though I do not like obscene material myself and choose not to read it or write it, I don't want the government putting its boot down on writers or artists, and let me add this to the pot, boys and girls—I don't want the government funding crap, either, and there has been a lot of crap the government has funded, so my message to the government is, Cut it out. If an artist wants to put a crucifix in a jar of urine, don't make me pay for that. Let that artist try to make it on his own and see how far he gets.

Al Bendich, then, unlike Bob Boyd, was the recipient of good timing. We cut to 1961 and a comic named Lenny Bruce was lacing his act with profanity, and he got cuffed and stuffed by the San Francisco police one night, and hauled into court, and guess who the judge was? Horn, again. And guess who Lenny Bruce hired? Al Bendich. Only this time Lenny Bruce insisted on a jury, which meant Al Bendich had to bring in an array of witnesses and work his butt off, but in the end the jury acquitted Lenny Bruce, too, and that's how Al Bendich struck another blow for the right to speak freely, which is a right we better not take for granted or get all huffy about when what somebody says is offensive to us, which is why these idiotic speech codes on college campuses and in workplaces, where if something you say "hurts" someone's "feelings" you can get booted out of school or fired, and that's not progress, friends, that's a return to the past, to the Inquisition, to the stake and kindling, to everything that Al Bendich and Allen Ginsberg and Lawrence Ferlinghetti fought against. And if that's that kind of wimpy, craven victim you want to populate our land for the foreseeable future, and beyond, then you just keep making "hurt feelings" the measure of what we can say or think.

I hope Al Bendich rests in peace, but he won't be so peaceful if this speech code fascism keeps up.

Rod Taylor died. He was 84. The *Los Angeles Times* notice called him "Legendary actor Rod Taylor," and while I liked Taylor quite a bit, he was not a legend. You pin the term *legend* on someone like Cary Grant or Clark Gable or Katharine Hepburn or Bette Davis. Rod Taylor was fine, a pretty good leading man in his day, but we're not writing books about him or going out to a theater for a Rod Taylor festival which, again, is not a knock on Rod. He was who he was and he did his best, and his best was pretty darn good, and what more can we expect out of ourselves and others? You get certain cards dealt to you, your DNA and your looks and your abilities and talents. Nobody gets the same cards. Some get a full house right away, like Grant, who was handsome and funny and charming all at once, not because he went to charm school or handsome school, but because he got those good cards dealt to him by the Dealer. Rod Taylor got a pretty high pair. He was good looking and a good actor, but he wouldn't beat Cary Grant at the legends' poker table.

. . .

What Taylor was was reliable, and that's a very good and honorable thing to be. Somebody who shows up on time and does his work, and does it well. Rod's most famous role was as the man in *The Birds,* in which Tippi Hedren gets all sorts of messed up by angry seagulls trying to take over the world. When we think of *The Birds* we usually don't think of Rod Taylor, but of those screaming schoolchildren running down the road as the seagulls fly over and peck the heck out of them. Rod Taylor was a good part of the story and he saved Tippi and that's not a bad legacy, because people will be watching *The Birds* forever.

Rod Taylor also played Travis McGee once, in a TV movie I believe it was. Travis McGee, of course, was the hugely popular series character created by John D. MacDonald, who made a mint off old Travis. Readers loved the character, who lived on a houseboat in Florida, who had a Jimmy Buffet style of life, and if you know anything about Jimmy Buffet you know he has these rabid fans who want to sit on beaches all day sipping Margaritas. The fans of McGee were like that, too, and even still are. There was always trouble getting a McGee movie project going, but Rod did it and was a pretty good McGee. At one time there was talk about Sam Elliott playing McGee, and that might have worked, although I don't quite see the laconic Elliott in that role.

By the way, I would love to come back someday as Sam Elliott's voice.

So Rod Taylor played the role of McGee and did a regular, workmanlike job, and that's a really good thing to have on a tombstone: *He did a workmanlike job, every time.* Be ye plumber or actor, lawyer or receptionist, singer or dancer, preacher or politician, writer or poet, cop or clown, carnival barker or dress designer—do your work and do it well, and while you may not become a legend you certainly will not be considered a fraud.

~

Michael D. White, 59, died at his home in Silver Spring, Md. That's too young to die, but we don't get to pick the timing or the cause (leaving out suicide, of course) which in the case of Michael D. White was chronic obstructive pulmonary disease.

The notice in the *Washington Post* says that Mr. White was a welder and sheet metal mechanic who had once been a small-arms repair technician in the Marine Corps. His labor, then, was what they used to call "good, honest work." The kind of work that makes other things possible, like building buildings or keeping alive on the battlefield. It's not glamorous, welding, it's not going to get you on a talk show, like actors who think too highly of themselves and also think that whatever comes out of their mouths is worth listening to, just because they command millions of dollars for sticking their face on a movie screen, a face that was given to them not by welding but by God, or a skilled surgeon, and therefore they think they can spout and spout even though they have not a thought in their head to speak of, because it has never been demanded of them that they do good, honest work in their own minds—those are the kinds of people who get on talk shows, not the welders and small arms technicians like Mr. Michael D. White of Silver Springs, Md.

. . .

But his kind of work, his kind of contribution, will last longer than the chuckleheads who think that fame trumps accomplishments, that a celebrity is worth more than any welder of the past, any riveter, any of those men and women in World War II who kept our boys outfitted in France and North Africa and Italy, who did their day's labor and ate out of lunch pails and came home and raised children and acted decently toward their neighbors.

Thank you, then, Michael D. White! Thank you, Rosie the Riveter! Not insipid, ye, not chuckleheaded or stupid but glorious in thy doings and workings, thy weldings and rivetings. Thank you for bridges and schools and ships and airplanes and cars and tables and barbecues. Thank you for being steady and strong.

Kim Fowley died at the age of 75. The *Times* called him "the mercurial and eccentric music producer and Svengali who created and managed the all-female rock group The Runaways in the 1970s."

Svengali is a character in a novel called *Trilby* published in the 1890s by a man named George du Maurier, who was the grandfather of Daphne du Maurier, who wrote the classic novel *Rebecca* and many other great stories (including the aforementioned *The Birds*). Svengali was a man who hypnotizes and seduces a girl he wants to turn into a famous singer. Calling someone a Svengali is calling them a puppet master who pulls someone's strings in the hope of monetary gain. In the book he is described as tall and bony, and "well-featured but sinister." This is also the look of many politicians.

. . .

To be *mercurial* is to be temperamentally unpredictable, to have highs and lows, to change moods on a dime. No one is sure where that word came from, whether it meant the Roman god Mercury, who was clever and changeable; or the planet Mercury, because people observed other people who were "born under the planet Mercury" were temperamentally unpredictable in their moods; or for the chemical element mercury, which slides all over the place and also changes according to heat.

Whatever the word and whatever his temperament, Kim Fowley must have had an eye for talent because one of the original Runaways was Joan Jett, who could rock and roll, and still does.

If you ever sit down and look at yourself—inwardly, I mean, not holding a mirror in front of your face—and think about your personal conduct (and the world would be a much better place if more people did this very thing) and can choose which way to go, don't be either *mercurial* or a *Svengali*. Mercurial adults are bad-tempered children who never grew up. Svengalis are narcissists who use other people. Don't do those things. Grow up. Treat people with respect. Remember that you're going to die someday and people will talk.

Yet people spend a lot of time *not* thinking about death. That is because most people prefer to stay alive. Not all people, of course. There is the sad fact of suicide which is usually undertaken when the pain of living becomes too much, and the chemicals in the brain have taken on a dark, cloudy appearance. But in otherwise healthy individuals, thinking about death is a downer, especially among the young. And even among the middle-aged, to use various pursuits and ingestions to keep from thinking dismal thoughts about their own demise. In the 1950s the preferred form of ingestion was the gin Martini, which is the only true Martini, by the way, not vodka, though the latter has now supplanted the gin Martini for no other reason than the continued demise of Western Civilization.

It wasn't always like this. Back in the hunting and gathering days, there wasn't much else to do but think about death. That's because death was always around the corner. Wild animals and other tribes who wanted to take what you had hunted and gathered, and maybe carry off your women and children, too. Death was on the line all the time, and that was how you got storytellers. Storytellers would help people not think about death. They would tell stories about heroes, create myths, to give the tribe a little hope that they could do the same thing as the heroes did, and survive and be victorious and stay alive.

I imagine the best of the storytellers would be rewarded by the king of the tribe. Maybe with a monthly stipend of fox furs. If the storyteller had someone else from the tribe secure the furs in return for storytelling, perhaps that other person kept 15% of the furs as a commission.

Things really don't change—so wrote Solomon, son of David, in *Ecclesiastes*. We still are born and live and die. In between birth and death is the place where we live well or ill. The in-between is where bravery and honor and nobility and love reside. To not pursue these before the end of days is a misstep. A good obituary reminds us of the time we have left.

∾

A TV director by the name of **Tony Verna** died at the age of 81. He is a prime candidate for coming back to life and living all over again, for he was the man who introduced something to the national television audience back in 1963, for the first time ever, a thing which revolutionized the way we watch and analyze sporting events—instant replay. It was during the Army-Navy football game, which in those days was a big deal and watched by most football fans. Which reminds me of an old joke I give to you now, to use on your friends and acquaintances. Whenever you are limping around because you've banged your knee and somebody says, "Hey, what's the matter?" you say, "It's an old Army injury." Pause. Then say, "I fell off a barstool during the Army-Navy game." This will please the crowd and you will thereafter be invited to a ton of parties.

So Mr. Verna gave us instant replay, which now prevents professional and college football games from being ruined by a bad call on the field in real time. It would be nice to have instant replay in our lives. For example when we make a social *faux pas* that wasn't really *faux* but everyone thinks it is because they heard it that way. You could say to them, "Wait! I didn't say that! I said *I love duck with orange sauce.* That's what I said!" And when they continue laughing you say, "Let's run back the tape, shall we?" And you could slow it down and show your lips moving to form certain sounds and not others, and that would be the end of that.

. . .

Instant replay is also the basis of time-loop stories. Those are stories where the protagonist goes back to the beginning of a sequence, over and over, living out that same sequence with the knowledge of what he learned in all the other sequences. Like *Groundhog Day.* It's an idea from Nietzsche, that we live in these ever-returning loops, which once prompted Woody Allen to say, "Great. That means I'll have to sit through the Ice Capades again."

It's always tough to make a time-loop movie and have it make sense. The Tom Cruise movie *Edge of Tomorrow,* based on the Japanese novel *All You Need Is Kill* by Hiroshi Sakurazaka, is one such example. It's a very entertaining movie with a great premise and excellent performances, but there is one, huge hole in the logic of the plot, and I'm not going to give it away here because I think you ought to watch the movie and enjoy it for yourself and then instant-replay it, at least the last ten minutes of it, to discern this plot hole, for which I have seen some ingenious justification attempts, none of which work.

Which is why endings are so important for a writer. A terrible ending can ruin an otherwise enjoyable read. Endings are hard. The hardest part of a novel for me. I can make up first chapters all day long, but wrapping things up at the end is no walk in the park, friend, because the ending has to be satisfying yet surprising; pleasing yet unpredictable. An ending can be happy, sad, or ambiguous, but it has to feel just right, and that's where some novelists of repute have a tough time, because some of them say they just think up a situation and write the book, but when they come to the end it seems a little, what's the word, contrived?

Well, what else can they do? They've painted themselves into a plot corner and the only way out is contrivance.

Other writers, mainly of the mystery and thriller type, like to know the ending up front, and then everything else can be worked into the plot with geometric logic, as Captain Queeg would have put it (Captain Queeg is a character in *The Caine Mutiny* by Herman Wouk, played by Humphrey Bogart in the movie. And he's a bit paranoid, but so are writers).

But writers tend to fall into two camps: the plotters and the pantsers. The plotters like to plan and outline and do a lot of work on the story before they start writing. Pantsers (short for "seat of the pants") just dive in and write and let things happen and follow their brain wherever it leads. I find that "pure" pantsing is too much of a time waster for me, so I plan much of the plot in advance.

Right now, however, with this book, I am pantsing the heck out of it, because there is no pattern, no plot, it's a record of what I'm thinking at the moment as I look at death notices, and I am finding out what I have to say as I go along, which is not something I recommend for social occasions because you cannot go back and edit social occasions, unless and until some future genius invents instant replay for real life, in which case you can then shoot your mouth off all you like. A fellow who could do that naturally was a man named George F. Kaufman.

.   .   .

Kaufman was a famous playwright and wit, part of the fabled Algonquin Round Table in New York. The Algonquin Hotel had a table in its restaurant. It was round. During the 1920s, several writers and humorists of the day would meet there regularly to eat, drink, joke around, and make snide remarks about people they wanted to take down a peg. Kaufman was one of the best at this and for that reason was one of the early writers for the Marx Brothers, especially Groucho, for whom peg-taking-down was practically a religion.

Kaufman went on to a storied Broadway career and kept his wit, which came in handy when another famed playwright, Clifford Odets (pronounced, Oh-DETS), came out with *Rocket to the Moon,* which was not science-fiction, but some drama about a dentist having an affair with his assistant, and what it lacked was the political activism of Odets's earlier work, which was noted by critics, especially George S. Kaufman, who wrote: *Odets, where is thy sting?*

That's what hanging out at the Algonquin Round Table could do for you. Today, the Algonquin still says it has the original round table sitting there, but I tend to doubt it. It sounds like a tourist magnet to me, pay a premium and get to sit where Dorothy Parker and Robert Benchley and Kaufman and Harpo Marx used to sit. Money talks, but not so well as the Round Table folks did in their heyday.

The St. Louis Post-Dispatch ran an obituary for one **Shirley Carlson**, no age given, but it said she was "baptized into the hope of Christ's Resurrection" which is a nice way to put it, for when it is the end of things, there are many ways of saying it that are not so lovely, such as, "She kicked the bucket" or "The groundhog is delivering her mail."

She's "pushing up daisies" is a little nicer, what with the flower imagery and all, but "taking a dirt nap" is gauche, and people deserve better unless they commit evil on Earth, in which case I don't really care what people say about them after they are dead, so long as they are really and truly dead, and not only "mostly dead" as Miracle Max would say.

Some people say the departed "bought the farm," which is an odd phrase, don't you think? How can you buy anything after you're dead, let alone a farm? I'm all for farmers and chickens and corn and wheat, but who wants to die in order to buy a place where you have to get up early and work hard all day? How is that going to a heavenly rest?

No one seems to know how this phrase got associated with death. Some think it goes back to soldiers serving in the military in World War I or II. You had a lot of farm boys going off to war back then, and they'd lie on their cots and tell their buddies how they just want to survive this action so they can go back home and buy a farm. And when they didn't make it, in deference to the dream, the buddies would shake their heads and say, "Well, he just went off and bought the farm." Which again makes no sense, unless they believed he was going to be a ghost who wanted to raise chickens.

. . .

It could be that if you think of a farm as a piece of land, and the soldier's grave as a piece of land, you might be able to squeeze a little more out of "he bought the farm," but he's not going to be raising chickens, he's going to be pushing up daisies, so I still don't get it.

What would be a dog euphemism for death? "Rover? He bit the tire." "Rex? Got the big tick bath."

So considering all that, I like "baptized into the hope of Christ's Resurrection" quite well, and the rest of Shirley Carlson's notice, to wit: *Beloved wife of Charlie Carlson for 60 years. Loving mother of Linda Schaefer, Sandy (Mark) Joseph and Debbie (Robert) Chasen. Dearest Grandma of Michelle, Kristen, Mark, Brittany, Kenny, Kevin and the late Gregory, Jr. Dear sister of Don (Shirley), Ronnie (Wanda) and the late Gary. Caring aunt and friend to many.*

Sixty years a loving wife! Charlie couldn't have asked for a greater gift in this life. And look at all the kids and grandkids (and, sadly, a grandchild who went before his time, but who Shirley is now lifting again, because, friends, God receives all children who die unto himself, but look also at that last one, a *friend to many* and that is a glory, to have friends, to be a friend to many, like George Bailey in *It's a Wonderful Life*, and that is exactly the kind of life Shirley Carlson had, even though all lives have their downs as well as ups, their tragedies as well as triumphs, but if in the end you are a friend to many and beloved by many, you have done well, friend.

Faith Seidenberg died at the age of 91, and that's a ripe old age to go if you have your wits still about you, and Ms. Seidenberg apparently did, for the cause of death was Parkinson's, not Alzheimer's; it was the body and not the mind that gave out. She was a lawyer, and I have a theory that lawyers and comedians have less Alzheimer's than other retired folks. Why? Because they each have to exercise their brains every day, to keep sharp, to stay ahead, and I offer as Exhibits A and B Mr. Carl Reiner and Mr. Mel Brooks, both legendary comedy writers and performers, and both of them still sharp at age 90 (actually, as I write this, Reiner is 92 and Brooks is 88, so that averages right out to 90 in my book). You see these two giving interviews and they are cracking wise and remembering everything. Groucho Marx was the same way, even after he had a terrible stroke that affected the speed of his delivery. He still had that twinkle in his eyes, and I saw that twinkle first hand when I sat in front of him at the re-release of *Animal Crackers*, which my friend Steve Stoliar was largely responsible for, which is why I got invited to the opening and got to meet Groucho and see that twinkle in his eyes.

Which is how I would like to be at 90: Twinkle Eyes.

So comedians, always thinking about the next wisecrack, exercise their heads, and so do lawyers, many of whom practice into their eighties and even nineties. When I was in law school, wanting to become a trial lawyer, there was a legend of the trial bar named Louis Nizer, probably the most famous lawyer in America at the time. His biggest cases were in the 1950s and '60s. But I heard he was going to court somewhere in Riverside, and I drove down there and sat in the courtroom and watched him, at the age of 82, doing battle with lawyers half his age.

Perhaps, then, we may plausibly think that she was mentally sharp right up to the time her body couldn't take it anymore, because not only was she a lawyer, she was a crusading lawyer at the time we needed those crusades. I like the fact that she was a graduate of the Syracuse Law School, for my own mother went to Syracuse University and that's why I always pull for their football team except when they play USC.

The *New York Times* obit described Ms. Seidenbergher as "Indomitable in her professional and private lives," for she became a licensed pilot at 64 and then flew to the North Pole. I love that. Never give up, never give in, live life and don't settle.

Faith Seidenberg became a lawyer for the poor, first as a public defender and then in partnership with Civil Rights lawyer William Kunstler. She was most famous for breaking up an all-male institution. The case involved a bar in New York's Greenwich Village called McSorley's Old Ale House, which at the time was a male-only establishment. No women allowed. The reason? Well, McSorley's argued that men were men and in a gathering of other men wanted to be free to say things that might offend women. The problem for McSorley's was that they were a public, not private, drinking spot, so Faith Seidenberg went to court over it and a judge agreed. Part of the judge's opinion said, "Outdated images of bars as dens of coarseness and iniquity and of women as peculiarly delicate and impressionable creatures in need of protection from the rough and tumble of unvarnished humanity will no longer justify sexual separatism."

So McSorley's had to open its doors to all and let the chips and brassieres fall where they may, and what happened is that the laws of nature took over. McSorley's got lots of publicity and business boomed, and women largely chose to stay away, voluntarily.

Frank Mazzola died. He was 79. Mazzola was a tough kid from the streets of L.A. who was hired as a gang consultant for the movie *Rebel Without a Cause*, starring James Dean. Mazzola taught Dean how to talk and walk, and ended up choreographing the famous knife fight in the film. He'd been a member of a gang called The Athenians and they ran around Southern California getting into fights, which seems quaint, since L.A. gangs are now lethal and trafficking in all sorts of bad things, which is how the world goes when left to raw nature—that is human nature—it goes down, down, down, people become worse, not better, it's a fact of history and life that if you don't have something big and powerful to restrain humanity they will do very bad things, and even worse things if they band together, like what happens with gangs and governments. Which was what old Jim Madison and old Johnny Adams and all those guys knew, which is why they made it so the government couldn't be all powerful, because there was a Constitution that told it what to do, and there were voters who could boot scoundrels out of office. But they said something else, just as important, just as crucial for your neighborhood, and that's basically this: We're going to leave you free to pursue happiness on your own, but you better attend to religion, at least the ethics part, the love your neighbor and do unto others part, because once that goes you only have the law to hold you back and you might not give two rips about the law. So teach your children to follow the morals of Jesus even if you yourself do not choose to follow the way of the Cross, for love and respect are as much a part of being a citizen as your right to vote.

That's why it was common in the 1950s, when your humble correspondent entered this world, for parents of all colors to send their children to Sunday School, even if they themselves did not go to church, because that was where ethics were planted so your child would not grow up to knock over liquor stores or steal cars or con old ladies out of their retirement money.

What the wisdom of the ages has taught, and what we seem to have forgotten, is that each of us is in one big knife fight with our own natures, and we have to do something to keep the bad side from stabbing the good side in the heart.

Frank Mazzola was born in 1935 and so was of a generation who knew that. He managed to fight his nature and quit gang life and become a respected film editor. He married and had four daughters and three grandchildren, a goodly number that must have brought him more joy than working with James Dean, who was a brooder and a bit of a pain to be around. Dean was a naturally gifted actor who was best when a director could rein him in a little, *rein* being the operative word because, as Mazzola described him, James Dean was like a "wild animal."

And speaking of animals, let's talk about bears. Young bears. Cubs. Because **Ernie Banks** died at the age of 83. He was the Hall of Fame shortstop who played his entire 19-year career with the Chicago Cubs, who have not been to the World Series since 1945, and haven't won the whole thing since 1908, which is long enough for the fans of the team to be called "longsuffering," a word that explains itself.

Banks was the first African American to play for the Chicago squad. It was a full six years after Jackie Robinson broke the color barrier in Major League baseball.

My dad was teammates with Jackie Robinson at UCLA. Here's the team photo. My dad is the catcher.

Jackie Robinson was one of the greatest athletes to ever grace our land. He played baseball, football, basketball, and ran track. He will always be remembered for grace under pressure, because it was no bed of roses, those first few years Robinson played in the majors, but he did not lash out, he did not give anyone reason to doubt, and most of all he did not embarrass himself off the field, which is a lesson many athletes—of any color—need to learn, especially the narcissistic rookies who go to Vegas and brag about all the money they're making and get drunk, and do all that before they've played a single down in the NFL, and then when they do play a single down it is not worth watching because he's so bad, so dreadful, and so are all the other downs he plays, and then when the season's over he's back to partying in Vegas and embarrassing himself off the field. Jackie Robinson never did that.

Neither did Ernie Banks, who had what they called a "sunny" disposition, meaning eternally optimistic and upbeat, which is a very hard thing to be when you play for the Chicago Cubs and never get a whiff of a World Series. But Banks loved baseball, loved playing it, and that's what the players of his era were like, they loved the game before it was a big, money-making, billion-dollar business where players chase the almighty dollar. Very few players play for the same team their whole careers. Banks was one of them. So was Hall of Famer Robin Yount, who I went to school with and played Little League with. Little League was a time of dreams, found and lost. I was not as great as I wanted to be. I always played with the idea that I could be Willie Mays or Don Drysdale. I knew all the players, especially the old ones, and Ernie Banks was one of them. I was into the history of the sport, knew all the members of the Hall of Fame and their stories. I wanted to have my own plaque hanging at Cooperstown.

It would start at Sunrise Little League, where the best player was Robin Yount. He was a natural athlete, naturally confident, which I was not. Robin made great plays at shortstop and pitched powerfully, and man he could hit. I was better than average but I didn't want to be average, I wanted to be great. My greatest thrill came when I was twelve, my last year in Little League, playing for the Red Sox. Robin played for the mighty Yankees, who had other standout players like Joe Medina and Steve Whitehead. They were fearsome. I had started the year like gangbusters, hitting two home runs in one game off Berk Baker, a great pitcher.

Then we played the Yankees. I came up to bat in a pressure situation, and Robin Yount was pitching. I was nervous about this, not confident, the butterflies in my stomach were all screaming like little Frank Zappas, the people in the stands were cheering and what a moment it was as I stepped to the plate.

The coach of the Yankees called time, went to talk to Robin Yount on the mound. The order was, walk Bell intentionally. Robin Yount, the best pitcher in the league, gave me an intentional pass! It was the high point of my baseball career, which ended the next year as I began to concentrate on basketball. But how many men can say they were intentionally walked by a Hall of Famer?

. . .

That's called putting the best spin on the things that happen to you, which is how Ernie Banks was all the way up to the end. He had a saying. When he got to the park, which was Wrigley Field —the Cubs played all their games during the day back then— Banks would say, "It's a beautiful day, let's play two!"

It's nice to be able to feel that way about what you're doing at any given moment, that you'd like to double up and play two.

And speaking of twos, there's *Playboy* magazine, which is known primarily for its literary quality. [Clears throat] What I mean is that **Alice K. Turner**, the fiction editor at that magazine for 20 years, died at the age of 75. She brought a measure of respectability, ahem, between the folds, as it were, or at least on either side of them. She published some of the best writers in America and discovered others, and was appreciated in-house because, of course, everyone knew that men bought *Playboy* for the articles and short stories.

Ms. Turner has given me a new quotation on writing, lifted from her obit in the *New York Times*. When I teach writing workshops I sometimes get a question along the lines of "Why should we have to learn about structure? Can't we just let the story happen naturally?"

I always say, Look, first learn what works, what has always worked, and know why it works. Then you can mess around all you want. And when your books don't sell you'll know how to fix them. Thus, I liked this Alice K. Turner quote:

"If you're good enough, like Picasso, you can put noses and breasts wherever you like. But first you have to know where they belong."

~

John Bayley died at the age of 89, and doesn't that number make you wish he'd made it just one more year? Ninety seems a goodly age if you're going to get as far as 89, so you might as well go for it. If you're going to go in your eighties I think 85 is a good number, right there in the middle. Of course it all depends on your body and your mind. Lingering while being enfeebled is not a happy way to go. The best way would be to drop right after you've completed a good and worthy task. Like Robert B. Parker, the prolific American crime writer, who was working on his next book when he died at his desk of a heart attack. He was 77. Or what about Bing Crosby, the famous crooner and Academy Award winning actor? He loved golf, and at the age of 74 played 18 holes at a beautiful course in Spain, and shot an 85, which is a great score for any amateur, especially one who is 74. After sinking his last putt to win a friendly match, he said to his buds, "It was a great game." Then he took a few steps and collapsed and died. There is an exit for you.

The other kind of death, the long and slow decline, is harder to watch when it is one you love, and especially when the vicious demon called Alzheimer's is doing its dirty work, and that's where John Bayley comes back into the story, for he was married for 40 years to the famous writer Iris Murdoch, who was as smart as they come, having studied philosophy at Cambridge, for goodness' sake, where the smartest people go to become smarter, and then she wrote deeply philosophical novels on the order of Dostoevsky, who was the leading hitter in the Big Leagues of philosophical novelizing. This amazing mind and talent fell to the demon Alzheimer's and she lingered for another five years, and John Bayley stayed by her as the chief caregiver, and that is an act of courage and love that many unsung brave lovers go through in these days of longer lives.

Life requires bravery and we don't do service to those we raise by building up expectations that all will be well and you don't have to fight your way through a jungle from time to time. You're not always going to be on the boat on the jungle cruise with a guide with a gun, like they have at Disneyland. There are going to be many times you're on your own out there, and all you'll have is courage, so teach your children what that means. It does not mean the absence of fear. It means feeling the fear and going forward anyway.

I'm sure there were many times when John Bayley feared the next day, when his wife as still alive but not there, and he loved her still.

Joe Franklin died. He was 88. He was a talker, a champion talker, the fellow they say invented the talk show, the first to sit at a desk and have guests, and boy did he have guests, like Marilyn Monroe early on, and Liza Minnelli. A lot of the guests were just getting started when they were on his show, people like Bruce Springsteen and Al Pacino and Dustin Hoffman.

I saw an early Springsteen concert, probably around the same time he was on the Franklin show, before he became big, became The Boss, and I thought he was only okay. I found it a bit of an act, his blue collar persona, and still feel that way, and I've never liked his voice. His music is okay (Clarence "Saxman" Clemons elevated everything), but his lyrics a bit pat. So there at the start of things I thought Mr. Springsteen was less than what his amazing press handlers said he was—I say amazing press because, I believe, he was on the covers of both *Time* and *Newsweek,* maybe the same week, and that made everybody say, *OK, this guy's the next big thing,* and that's what he became. But part of thinking for yourself is not accepting the next big thing just because a magazine or newspaper say it is. At least you should be able to talk about it rationally, though many so-called *fans* are not rational, for the word *fan* is short for *fanatic.*

I never watched Joe Franklin, but it is impressive that he never missed a show in 60 years. If you want to be impressed with someone, be impressed with that, because that record is like Lou Gehrig and Cal Ripkin impressive, the two gentlemen who played the most consecutive major league games without sitting out because of a twisted ankle or bad thumb.

You've got to be able to play your game and sometimes you have to play hurt. Good job, Joe, who is now interviewing Anita Ekberg and Ernie Banks.

Charles Townes died. He was 99. He almost made it to the century mark, but 99 is close enough to be astounding and admirable. But even more astounding and admirable is what Charles Townes did with his mind. He invented the laser, for one thing. He won the Nobel Prize. He also thought about spiritual matters. And like a huge number of advanced physicists he determined that the universe had a beginning that needed a First Cause.

Which pretty much rules out dogmatic atheists. In point of fact, dogmatic atheists rule themselves out, for it is impossible to rationally claim there is no God. Michael Shermer, a very popular atheist, admits this. He calls himself a "soft" atheist, because there is no way he can say with certainty there is no God. He just has decided there's not enough evidence for him, which still doesn't do justice to the term a-theist. Mr. Shermer is, rather, a strong agnostic.

To be an atheist these days requires too much faith. To be an agnostic is to ignore too much evidence, the kind that Nobel Prize winner Charles Townes saw, and that another leading physicist named Robert Jastrow noted, and the one thing you can't throw at these guys is that they were stupid.

It was Jastrow who came up with the best quote of all, in his book *God and the Astronomers:*

"For the scientist who has lived by his faith in the power of reason, the story ends like a bad dream. He has scaled the mountain of ignorance; he is about to conquer the highest peak; as he pulls himself over the final rock, he is greeted by a band of theologians who have been sitting there for centuries."

Charles Townes not only knew you can't be a rational atheist. He made the case that you can hardly be a strong agnostic.

And there's a practical reason not to be an agnostic. Because you don't want your headstone to read: *All dressed up and nowhere to go.*

Colleen McCullough died. She was 77. She was the author who burst into international fame with *The Thorn Birds,* which took off and was made into a mini-series which she reportedly hated. That's an old story, an author not liking what the movie makers do with her book, but then writers are at the low end of the totem pole in Hollywood. At the top of the pole are the suits and the bean counters, the ones who usually know less than the writers about what makes a good story and what should be done with it on the screen. But it's all about the money and the control, and what William Goldman said. Goldman is one of the legendary screenwriters (*Butch Cassidy and the Sundance Kid; All the President's Men*) and he observed of the suits in Hollywood: "Nobody knows anything. ... Not one person in the entire motion picture field knows for a certainty what's going to work. Every time out it's a guess and, if you're lucky, an educated one."

. . .

That's art for you, and despite what Ms. McCullough thought of it, the TV version of *The Thorn Birds* was a big, huge, undisputed hit, starring Richard Chamberlain as the priest who loves Rachel Ward, and that's not hard to understand at all, and vice versa, because Richard Chamberlain was in those days a good-looking fellow, having made his name as a heartthrob of '60s teenagers in the television show *Dr. Kildare.* I had a passing knowledge of all this because I played Little League baseball one season with Richard Chamberlain's nephew, and one of the coaches was Richard Chamberlain's brother, and as I recall he was even better looking than Richard, even though he wasn't an actor, so that family had the genes going on for sure, which can be a blessing and a curse, and was a bit of millstone for Richard because he was not taken seriously as an actor.

I do recall when he got off the *Dr. Kildare* show he went over to England and studied acting in the legit theater, and at the time I thought that a pretty gutsy move, because he could have stayed here and gotten on another TV show, a sitcom maybe, and made tons of money. But Richard Chamberlain wanted to be a real actor, and the theater was where real actors hung out, and when he came back to America he started doing Shakespeare and classics and was very good.

Which is what I try to do as a writer, indeed, which is why I am writing this very book, to set up a challenge and do some stretching, and it's what I advise all who wish to write—honor your craft, and work at it, and you will become the better for it.

·　·　·

Richard Chamberlain was the better for his training, and turned in some really good performances, like *Shogun* and *The Three Musketeers* and *The Man in the Iron Mask* and as Allan Quatermain in *King Solomon's Mines* which I thought was better than most critics did.

So maybe Ms. McCullough should have cut the TV version some slack, because it was pretty good and brought her a ton of extra money from all the books sold as a result.

We spend too much of our lives complaining about things— things we can't change, things we shouldn't want to change, things that don't matter that much, and what happens as a result of all that negative expulsion? You get wrinkles. Not a good exchange. Instead of complaining, get lost in a book like *The Thorn Birds* or *The Executioner: War Against the Mafia*. The former is a big, long romance, the latter a vigilante revenge story. Between these two is a whole universe of genres, and that's nothing to complain about.

Jack Leggett died. He was a ripe old 97. The *New York Times* said he was "a friend to writers," and that is a very fine thing to be, a friend to a particular group with whom you walk, talk, teach, fellowship, complain, hope, dream, motivate, and occasionally pick up the check for. Jack Leggett earned that sobriquet by being the longtime head of the Iowa Writers Workshop, which in literary circles is like New York for actors, or Hamburger University for McDonald's managers.

. . .

It's perhaps the most prestigious of the MFA programs, the Big Kahuna, and Jack Leggett was a friend to the writers there. And I have absolutely no doubt that Mr. Leggett was a dedicated Yoda to the legions of Skywalkers seeking to become literary Jedi.

There's a lot of flapping of gums and clacking of keyboards over the worth of MFA degrees, and you'll find all manner of disgruntled alumni, ticked-off failures, and ghastly stories of inflated-ego profs taking out their own failings and frustrations on hapless young charges who think these people actually know what they're talking about when it comes to fiction, which is not always the case, because fiction is not any one thing and there are plenty of successful doers and failed doers who cannot teach, that's always been so.

There is a legendary putter-downer who is so infamous at the put-down game that he inspired a play called *Seminar*, which I saw on Broadway starring **Alan Rickman**. Rickman played a haughty, failed writer who paid back the universe by making young writing students suffer, by telling the talented ones they had no talent and also plucking the young females for a roll in the hay. Rickman, of course, was one of our finest actors (he died in 2016, and thus is not a subject for this book, which cuts off on December 31, 2015, though I am bolding his name for his much deserved and appreciated cameo here), and he was perfect for the role, because you can hear the sneer in his voice, that tonal Brit accent dripping with sarcastic honey. The play was clever, and in the end turned into a nice, redemptive ode to the love of writing and the writing life. Which is not always how it comes out in the real world.

. . .

The writing life, by the way, is not a generous jolt of frosting spelling out your name, let me tell you. There's a lot of cake you have to bake, too, and it can get hot in the kitchen. So if Mr. Leggett was a real friend to writers, then God bless him. And to writers who are thinking of going for an MFA, I hope you find a friend like that and then find a way to sell your writing so you can pay off your student loan.

What we really need is a commercial MFA program, a place that'll teach writers how to write prose that sells like crazy, because "literary fiction," so-called, is the kind that sells hardly at all, even if it manages to get published these days, which it usually doesn't. To really help writers make bank we should teach them plot and structure and dialogue and scenes, not just pretty sentence making, like stringing one pearl at a time on a necklace nobody is going to wear, let alone buy. I've written several books for writers, so aspirants can get a pretty good education in commercial fiction for only about thirty or forty bucks.

Writers should study their craft, get feedback from people who know what they're talking about and then write some more. You can do that without paying tens of thousands of dollars, dollars better spent on fine wine, movies, charity, a new car, a fedora, a George Foreman grill, a Total Gym, a Moka coffee maker, a night on the town with your love, and, of course, books.

Rod McKuen died. He was 81. To a generation of flower children, hippies of the late '60s and '70s, rainbow-believing, hands-across-America hoping, doobie-burning, bell-bottoms wearing, optional-bathing, star-gazing, Vietnam-war resisting youth, Rod McKuen was the poet laureate, the most commercially successful poet the world has ever seen, and it hasn't seen many, for poetry is not the thing to go into if one hopes to gain the long green.

But Rod McKuen wrote a hit song for a movie called *The Prime of Miss Jean Brodie*, and then started putting out verses in book form, with titles like *Listen to the Warm* and *We Touch the Sky*, and that's when Rod McKuen knew he had a winning formula on his hands, said formula eventually landing him in a huge mansion in Beverly Hills.

His poetry was never going to give Tennyson or Keats a run for the prestige, but it was innocuous enough, it didn't hurt anyone, it sang softly of lovely things, even if such things were about as likely to occur as a unicorn in your garden, so I hope Rod enjoyed his fame and fortune, for those are two things most poets never see.

According to his obit, McKuen actually started as a Beat poet, hanging out in beatnik bars with the likes of Jack Kerouac and Neal Cassady, the Beats being all about be-bop prose rhapsody, as Kerouac put it, and Kerouac himself was the chief Beat, writing two books that made him famous, *On the Road* and *The Dharma Bums*, but after that he did not live a beautiful existence, drinking himself to death. McKuen cashed in his Beat credentials when he went for the commercial market. He lived much longer than Kerouac, but Kerouac is better known and keeps getting rediscovered by each new generation of college male. And there's a tradeoff for you, one many writers have faced: do I stay true to my art, even though it doesn't sell, or write what will sell and hope I remain happy about it?

Some writers of the past tried to do both, using a fake name, called a pen name, for the stuff that made money. Evan Hunter was such a writer, a man who wanted to be taken seriously as an American author, and put those hopes into novels like *The Blackboard Jungle* and *Strangers When We Meet*. But to put steak on the table he wrote for the "ghetto" of the time, the paperback originals market, the world of hard-boiled cops and PIs and dames and roscoes. He wrote those books as Ed McBain, and that doppelgänger took off, McBain did, earning Evan Hunter millions of dollars but leaving Mr. Hunter a bit disgruntled that his made-up self was more famous and even more highly regarded as a writer. Heck, even today if you type in Evan Hunter you get taken to the Ed McBain Wikipedia page. What a kettle of fish that must have been for Evan!

The **Seattle Seahawks** Super Bowl bid died. It died on the one-yard line with under a minute to play. They had the ball and the ballgame in their hands, three plays and a timeout in their pocket, and in their backfield a runner known as "Beast Mode," which tells you what kind he is, the kind who can smash a ton of human flesh backward at least 36 inches, and then it came, the call, the play, the blunder, the mistake that will be talked about as long as there are Super Bowls—inexplicably the Seahawks ran a *pass play,* which is a play in which there is a pass, which means that there is a possibility that the other team—which is under no obligation to allow you to run your pass play successfully—has the opportunity to *intercept your pass* and take the ball away and all your hopes and dreams—and that is exactly what happened. The New England Patriots took the ball away and there went the ballgame, and on that play so many things changed.

The quarterback of the Seahawks, a talented young man named Russell Wilson, had the chance to go legend, to become talked about in storied terms. Instead, he throws an inaccurate pass that is picked off.

The other quarterback, Tom Brady, vilified as a cheater for deflating footballs, cements his place as perhaps the greatest quarterback of all time.

This one play affected the legacies of two coaches. The Pats coach, Bill Belichick, had also been vilified as a cheater. Another legendary coach by the name of Don Shula even publicly called him "Belicheat." This one play gave him a place on the Rushmore of NFL coaches.

Pete Carroll, on the other hand, who could have started jackhammering his Rushmore spot, instead has this one mistake hung around his neck for the rest of his career. I have called it Carroll's Call, and compared it to another notorious mistake some baseball old-timers still talk about today—Merkle's Boner.

By the way, *boner* was for most of its history a word for "big mistake." Just so young readers know.

. . .

It happened way back in 1908, but because it decided a pennant race, it is ensconced in the trophy case of sports history. Fred Merkle was a rookie with the New York Giants and they were playing the Chicago Cubs with the National League championship on the line. Merkle was about to become one of the heroes, for in the bottom of the ninth inning, with the score tied 1-1, and two outs, Fred Merkle zinged a single, sending his teammate, Moose McCormick, to third. So the winning run was only 90 feet away!

Lo and behold, the next batter, Al Birdwell, sends a single to center field. McCormick crosses home plate. Pandemonium! The crowd starts pouring onto the field.

And Fred Merkle, thinking that the game was over, stopped running and never touched second base. He turned and jogged to the dugout.

Well, friends, there was a little rule in place that said you can't get a scoring run where a third out is made by a force play on a runner. Merkle was that force play.

The Cubs' second baseman, Hall of Famer Johnny Evers, was smart enough to know the rule. And he somehow got hold of the baseball (or a substitute, for in the chaos the original ball may have been tossed to the fans) and ran out and touched second, then appealed to the umpires that the rule was in play and the run did not score!

· · ·

Well, Evers won that appeal. It was upheld by the league. The game had to be replayed. And the Giants lost. And poor Fred Merkle had "Merkle's Boner" sewed to his chest for the rest of his life. I think Carroll's Call will pretty much be the same for the Seahawks coach.

All this, based on one bad play call. Which shows, again, not only the fleetingness of glory, but the remorselessness of life, how it giveth and taketh away, and therefore how we must be prepared to take the good with the bad, the sweet with the sour, the Abbott with the Costello, and more than that, move on, refuse to be beaten even after a boneheaded mistake of epic proportions is on your resume.

Pete Carroll used to coach at USC, and their song, very simply, says, "Fight on!"

Do it, Coach.

Edward J. Saylor died at age 94. He was, according to the *New York Times*, "one of the last surviving members of the Doolittle Raiders, a band of World War II airmen who bombed Japan in early 1942, stunning the Japanese at a time when their army and navy were racking up victories across Asia." The attack was credited with getting in the head of Japan, as it were, and boosting morale at home in America.

. . .

He was part of that rapidly disappearing Greatest Generation, the one that fought in World War II and gave us the freedom and autonomy we enjoy today but refuse to teach in our schools anymore. Yes, that's true, it's not acceptable to mention things like freedom and liberty and *In God We Trust*, for that implies we are somehow "better" than Russia or Iran, and we certainly don't want to hurt their feelings or ever imply that our way of life may actually be better for actual people. Far be it from us to do that! Even though it's not just true, it's *freaking* true. Maybe someday we can recover our brass, our American spirit, and be proud of it.

Sergeant Edward Saylor believed in something else that is not taught anymore—sacrifice. For a greater good, for a greater mission, for the good of the Earth. For on this mission over Japan Saylor did not expect to survive. But he volunteered for it. He knew what he was fighting for. And he almost didn't make it.

This is the stuff of a Hollywood movie: Saylor's plane ran out of fuel and ditched into the China Sea. With his life raft rapidly deflating, Saylor and some crew mates managed to make it to a Chinese island. There, villagers helped hide them from Japanese troops. The villagers moved the men into a cave, then into a Buddhist temple, and even under the wet mats of a fishing boat. Finally, Saylor and the others got to safety and back home.

For this, Saylor received the Distinguished Flying Cross.

God bless men and women like Edward Saylor.

· · ·

When my dad was twenty-four years old he was a Lt. Commander on a ship in the South Pacific, fighting the Japanese empire. I find it hard to imagine a twenty-four-year-old today having the background, guts, competence, willingness, or education to do that very same thing. Yes, they can do it on Xbox, but I'm talking about the world, where bad guys live.

Carl Boldt died. The title of his obituary was: *Carl Boldt, teammate of Bill Russell in NCAA title run, dies at 82*. It is a "second place" type of obituary, a shared headline, because there are not very many Bill Russells, and if you happen to play with one, he will elbow his way into your obit.

If you don't know who Bill Russell was, I will give you the short version of a very tall man. He was 6'9" and perhaps the greatest defensive basketball player of all time. Utterly dominant. He went from the University of San Francisco to the Boston Celtics, and played his whole career there, and helped make the Celtics the most successful team of their time. They kept beating my Lakers, it was frustrating as all get out, because of Bill Russell and teammates like Bob Cousy and Satch Sanders and K.C. Jones and Sam Jones and Tommy Heinsohn. Bill Russell is a Mount Rushmore NBA player.

That was who Carl Boldt was teammates with, and Boldt had been an outstanding 6'5" forward in high school and even got drafted into the NBA, but never played there. He went on to coach basketball and then do other business things, and that's because as good as Boldt was, he was not as good as Bill Russell, in part because he was not as tall nor as quick, and that's just a matter of your DNA, the genes you get, but if you want to play the game you do your best with what you've got, and you can't let other people who are better than you stop you, because if you did that, well, maybe Wellington would not have gone up against Napoleon, maybe Crazy Horse would have figured Custer had it all going on, maybe the 1980 U.S. Hockey Team would have said, Hey, let's just accept that the Soviets can't be beat and be happy with the Silver Medal.

No, baby, you play and play hard and love what you do, and do it the best you can, and let those other chips fall where they may. There it is again. Can't get those chips metaphors out of my system.

I am a writer, and I do not consider myself as natively talented as Mr. Stephen King or Ms. Harper Lee, or any of a number of other writers, but I love what I do and I try to do it the best I can, every time out, and that includes this book you are reading now.

Charlie Sifford died. He was 92. The first African American to earn a PGA card, he was often called "the Jackie Robinson of golf." But it was a lot harder for Charlie Sifford, because he didn't have a Branch Rickey backing him up. He had to try to break through the color barrier all by himself. He was 39 years old when it finally happened. He had a long way to go to get there.

. . .

He started out as a kid, caddying at an all-white country club in North Carolina. On Mondays, when the club was closed, he'd sneak on the course and play. He developed a short swing and fast style of play because, he said, he was trying to keep from being caught and thrown off the grounds.

So he was not taught, unlike the kids of the club members. He just went out and learned by doing, and when he got on the PGA Tour he had to endure the catcalls of the gallery and even death threats.

Yet he persevered, and won a couple of times on the tour.

And he smoked cigars. Big cigars. Right out there on the course. And that was a good thing, for there was a time when men smoked cigars proudly, like my dad, and that was a time when America became great. But when cigars started going out of style the country went into decline. You do the math. Same thing with fedoras. When men stopped wearing fedoras (this was largely the fault of John F. Kennedy, who didn't wear a hat like Eisenhower did, so all the men who wanted to be cool like JFK didn't wear hats anymore) America started getting worse. Here is a bit of history that I am giving you, that you will not hear in college classrooms: When Jack Webb played Joe Friday on the old black-and-white *Dragnet* show, he wore a fedora. There was law and order in America. The show went off the air for a while. When Jack Webb brought it back in the late '6os, it was in color and Joe Friday no longer wore a fedora. And crime was more rampant on the streets.

·   ·   ·

You can look it up.

So Charlie Sifford smoking cigars and breaking the color barrier made America a better place.

The great sports writer Jim Murray wrote about Sifford in the Los Angeles Times, back in 1969:

"Charlie birdied, not talked, his way through social prejudice. He broke barriers by breaking par. His weapon was a 9-iron, not a microphone. Charlie stands as a social pioneer not because he could play politics, but because he could play golf."

Lizabeth Scott died. She was 92, and that was surprising, for I thought she was long dead. Scott was one of the great femme fatales of film noir, and they never ended up in a good place, like at the end of *Too Late For Tears* where Lizabeth, a cold-hearted, money-loving, murdering woman falls off a balcony and splats to death around the bills she worked so criminally to procure. So hard was she in this movie that another great noir icon, Dan Duryea, was bested by her cold machinations, even when he started out as the guy who was going to use her to get the money. At one point he looks at her with a kind of sleazy awe and says, "Don't ever change, Tiger. I don't think I'd like you if you had a heart."

. . .

Lizabeth Scott had a smoky voice and feline features, as if she were Lauren Bacall's younger sister. She didn't have the acting range of Bacall, and her career came to a rather abrupt end when film noir died, while Bacall kept making movies and doing Broadway, which is how it goes sometimes, the landscape dries up and your farm goes under so you must do something else, move away or subdivide, and Lizabeth moved on, retiring from movies and I never knew what she did after that. I assumed she'd gone to that hazy nightclub in the sky in the 1980s.

But no. She kept living life, and doing good with it. According to the *New York Times* obit, she "led a quiet, largely private life. She helped raise funds for museums, art galleries and charities, including hemophilia research and hunger, and turned down many requests for interviews and guest appearances. There were rumors in the 1960s that she might marry Hal B. Wallis, the producer who discovered her, but she remained single."

Married or single, you have a choice to do good or not do it, and if you choose not you will sooner or later slip into a pit of desp...*cough cough, hack hack*...pit of despair, because you can't avoid it, it's in our wiring, and is meant to be, because it's a clue to where we came from, and where we are going, and what we are meant to do with our lives, and a big part of that is doing good for others.

Lizabeth Scott was to be suspected and feared in the movies. But she is to be respected and admired in death.

Norm Drucker died. He was 94 and could have died long ago, for he was an NBA referee in the early years of the league and fans could get unruly then, and threatening. There was little security in the arenas, and Norm Drucker and his fellow refs would often come out onto the court with their belts wrapped around their hands just in case some fan decided to get physical.

Time went on and the game developed, and then a giant named Wilton Norman Chamberlain came into the league, over 7 feet tall and with shoulders that were the size of small referees. So dominant was Wilt the Stilt (he actually hated that name, preferring another sobriquet, The Big Dipper) in those days that one season he averaged—averaged, mind you—50.4 points a game, a record that will never be equaled. In one game he scored 100 points, meaning he could have been shut out the next game and still averaged 50 points per. During that season, which was 1961-62, Chamberlain played every minute of every game. Except one. That was the one where the 5'11" Norm Drucker—no relation to Mort Drucker, the legendary cartoonist for *Mad* magazine—leveled two technical fouls on Wilt Chamberlain, which meant he got tossed from the game.

What happened was Wilt got called for a foul by another ref named Earl Strom, and Wilt complained a little too much and a little too colorfully, and got hit with a technical from Strom. Wilt decided then to bring Strom's mother into the conversation, and also said Strom must be betting on the game. Drucker heard that and slapped Wilt with his second T, and the Big Dipper was out. He did not go quietly, so Drucker hit him with a third technical.

. . .

Good for Drucker. He should have been around in Wilt's personal life to assess him 20,000 technical fouls for his treatment of women. For later in his life Wilt Chamberlain claimed that he had slept with 20,000 women over the years, a particularly male type of braggadocio that was in fashion back then, when Wilt was a frequent guest at the Playboy mansion where a man named Hugh Hefner walked around in silk pajamas, surrounded by women he called "bunnies" and living a life of pure, physical indulgence. Then someone calculated that for Wilt to have hit that number, during his potent years, he would have had to be averaging two or three a night, and that would not have left time for him to dunk any basketballs.

It was a dumb statement and a dumb way to spend a life, unless you believe life has no ultimate meaning and yourself no ultimate destination, which is a bad bet, for the wheel is spinning and you've got everything on Red 13.

Ethan Bendickson died in North Dakota. He was eight months old. His death was reported in the obituaries of the *Bismarck Tribune*, and he had his parents with him when his too-short life ended. The cause of death was not given, but it hardly matters, for the death of a baby is always tragic no matter how it happens. All babies deserve their shot in life, and it would be nice if there was an equal playing field, but the world is not set up that way as we know, and babies and children die, and parents grieve, and sometimes wonder, *Where is my child now?*

.   .   .

I will tell you where. I will tell you because it needs to be unequivocal and without nuance. It needs to be clear, for there has been a strain of theology that flows from Augustine, which holds that all of us, even while floating in amniotic fluid, are stained with the guilt of Adam, which means that our souls are going to Hell, directly to Hell, they will not pass Go, they will not collect $200. As this doctrine developed after Augustine, the church said to parents, Hey, you better baptize this little one right away or he'll die with this sin, and he won't go to Heaven and boom, you have the appearance of infant baptism.

Time went on, and people got upset over thinking of unbaptized infants going to Hell, so some priests came up with the idea of Limbo, which was a place short of Hell but not in Heaven where these unbaptized babies could go and spend eternity.

What the Bible actually teaches is that infants are innocent, completely, and I'm not going to write a 200-page treatise on this right now. You can study it out yourself. The conclusion is what I'm interested in, and that is the clear and unmistakable teaching that babies who die go to the presence of the Lord, and will stay there for eternity.

There is no Limbo, except on certain islands like Puerto Rico where it is a dance, not a dwelling. There is no Adamic sin that condemns an infant. If you care to go into it, start with a good, hearty study of the character of God. Because of God's character and because of the Scriptures, here is what can be said without qualm: Ethan Bendickson is with the Lord now, and will be with him forever.

Val Fitch died. He was 91, a Nobel Prize winner in physics, and the headline of his obit said he was the one who "discovered the universe to be out of balance."

I could have told him that. All you have to do is watch TV and you'll figure it out in no time.

But apparently, when you get to physics, there's something odd about our cosmos. The collision of matter and anti-matter has not destroyed everything like it should have. So Val Fitch set about to think this over, and proved there had to be some slight exception in the laws of physics in order for us to be here. But where did that exception come from? Why here? Why in such a way as to allow us to exist?

What many physicists now believe is that this exception is not a chance thing. It is, instead, evidence that we are not accidental byproducts of random occurrences, and that our universe was very clearly designed, and that to put any other spin on this evidence requires even greater faith than your average monk on a mountaintop.

In his statement accepting the Nobel, Fitch wrote, "At any one time there is a natural tendency among physicists to believe that we already know the essential ingredients of a comprehensive theory. But each time a new frontier of observation is broached we inevitably discover new phenomena which force us to modify substantially our previous conceptions. I believe this process to be unending, that the delights and challenges of unexpected discovery will continue always."

One could add that this is also a clue to existence: we aren't as smart as we think we are, though we're pretty good, and certainly we are not as smart as the Designer who put us here.

Brian Williams' credibility died. It was 22 years old. That's when Williams went to work at NBC News, as the weekend anchor. Later he moved into the lead chair. But then he got caught in a lie about his wartime experiences, for all news hounds of his age idolize the late Walter Cronkite, who showed up in an army helmet on battlefields, and became the "most trusted man in America" during the Vietnam war. So Williams exaggerated, or made up, a story about being hit by fire while in a helicopter during the Iraq conflict. The truth caught up with Williams, who could have been designed by Disney as an audio-animatronic robot of the quintessential news anchor—perfect hair, a face that never moved except the lips, a mellifluous voice. He had it all, did Williams, he was making millions talking to the American people five nights a week, as well as pushing his talented daughter in her show biz career.

So why did he inflate? Why did he play act? Why did that cool, unflappable mug issue convincing sounding untruths?

.   .   .

The ego, that creature that dwells within our electronic circuits, must be fed, unless we tame it and toss it kibble instead of red meat. There is a healthy ego and there is a voracious ego, and that was what caught up with Mr. Brian Williams, as it does with anyone who lets it out of its cage to roam free.

Oversized egos are part of the American landscape, and may even be charming if enough time goes by. But if they think they can get away with anything, very little charm is left.

In the late ′90s we had a guy here in California named Sybert who ran for the state Assembly. He was a Harvard man, a lawyer, and made money as a toy company executive. His opponent was a guy named Strickland.

One day Strickland came out and accused Sybert of running around tearing down his signs in the dead of night. Sybert denied it. He said he was home in bed with his wife that night. He tried to crack a joke: "At least she thought that man in bed with her was me!"

Two days later, Strickland produced a video of Sybert, on that very night, tearing down the signs and driving off in a car with the plates showing. The plates were traced to Sybert's registration.

D'oh!

.   .   .

So Sybert was forced to go before cameras and admit he lied, that it was a stupid thing to do, yadda yadda. He got his butt roundly and justifiably kicked in the election.

～

Jerry Tarkanian died. He was 84, and a legendary basketball coach, primarily at the University of Nevada at Las Vegas. He looked like a mafia don, which is one reason they called him Tark the Shark. He was Vegas royalty, because he was a winner. Sure, he consorted with a gambler or two. And yes, many of his athletes did not exactly complete their academic work. Maybe Vegas was really the exact place a guy like that needed to be.

There are people who charge through life with their teeth, chomping everything in their way. Tarkanian was like that. That's why he always chewed on a towel. If he didn't he would have chewed his way through people, buildings, and bureaucrats. He hated the NCAA. He sued them, even though a lot of what he did at Las Vegas was questionable.

Then there are the careful people, the ones who pause and consider and think things through. For a lot of my younger years I was the careful kind. I didn't want to make mistakes. I didn't take many risks. I looked around at classmates, especially in high school, who did risky things, and some of them ended up dead. One of them was a guy named Jim Caruso. I played basketball with him at Taft High School.

. . .

Caruso. He was a year ahead of me and clearly not wired the same as I was. I was dedicated to being an athlete. I didn't smoke, drink, party or stay up late. Caruso was the exact opposite.

To give you a picture, we were once playing in a winter league at another high school. We all drove our cars over to Pacific Palisades on Wednesday nights, played, and then drove home. To get there and back we had to take twisty Sunset Boulevard.

So I was driving back once after a game. It was a cold night in the canyon, and I carefully guided my Ford Maverick along Sunset. Suddenly, a convertible comes tearing by me. I don't remember who was driving, but I do remember who was in the passenger seat: Caruso, a cigarette in one hand and a beer in the other, his sweaty blond hair blowing in the wind. I remember he was laughing.

The thing was, Caruso had all this natural athletic talent. He was about six feet tall and built like a bull. And that's how he played basketball. He had one speed, full, and I don't think he ever took a shot that looked the same as any other. He was at his best when driving the lane and jumping in the air...then figuring out what to do once he was up there. Which was usually something very cool that either ended up with the ball going through the hoop or off the wall.

This drove our coach, John Furlong, absolutely crazy. Furlong was a strict disciplinarian and team-oriented coach. He yelled a lot. He got red-faced mad at you if you messed up too badly. None of us wanted to be on the wrong side of Coach Furlong.

Except Caruso. He just didn't seem to care. No matter how mad Furlong got at him, Caruso would take it silently, then go out on the floor and pretty soon do the same thing again. Which was why Furlong wouldn't start him. But he couldn't keep him on the bench for long because, despite everything, Caruso was too good not to be in the game, scoring points and grabbing rebounds. And sometimes frustrating the rest of us, because we'd be open for a fifteen footer while Caruso drove in against three or four players and tried to score by himself. Which he often did.

As frustrating as he was, it was impossible not to like him. He had this infectious smile and he seemed to go through life with a certain damn the torpedoes, full speed ahead kind of joy. He didn't do too well in his classes, but that didn't bother him. There was too much living to do to get caught up in the niceties of chemistry or calculus.

Whenever we'd play pickup games in the off-season, Caruso and I would try to get on the same team, because we knew we each had an iron will to win. In those days, in a crowded gym, the only way you got to keep playing was if your team won. Otherwise, you'd have to sit and wait in line for another turn. Besides that, Caruso was just flat out fun to play with in those games. He'd be laughing and joking and talking smack and shooting and rebounding and slapping you on your butt when you did something good.

. . .

Jim Caruso graduated (at least, I think he did) in my junior year. The next year we had another great team at Taft, this one disciplined and predictable, much to the relief of Coach Furlong. Still, I couldn't help feeling our team lacked a certain, what's the word, exuberance? I missed seeing Caruso cutting through the key, doing his thing, a thing uniquely his own.

Then one Saturday I was in the gym shooting around and a fellow teammate came in.

"Hey," he said, "did you hear about Caruso?"

I stopped shooting. "No, what?" I figured he was in jail or something, maybe picked up on a DUI.

"He's dead," my friend said.

I just stared at him, stunned.

"Killed in a car accident," he explained.

And I immediately thought of that night I saw Caruso in that convertible, and thought maybe this wasn't such a shock after all. I never got the details of the accident. I don't know whose fault it was. But it was, looking back, both sad and oddly predictable.

· · ·

I don't know what was going on in Jim Caruso's life. The only thing we had in common was basketball. It was enough. I didn't want to emulate his off the court antics. What I did want to do was, when the situation was right, go for the wild shot, the totally improvised move, just to see what happened. I knew you couldn't play a whole game that way, but you at least needed to have that kind of fearlessness in your arsenal. That's what it was Caruso had: pure fearlessness and trust in his abilities.

I draw an analogy to writing here. Discipline, fundamentals and hard work are still the keys, but you have to be willing to "go for it" sometimes. You have to jump in the air and figure out what to do when you're up there.

I still have this indelible picture of Jim Caruso. It was in a pickup game, the first time I'd ever played with him, before I came to Taft. His name had been whispered to me. Everybody knew about Caruso. I was a little bit intimidated by the prospect of playing with him. But then we started the game and I remember just watching him, marveling at his natural ability. Crunch time came and the game was tied and we needed a basket to win. Caruso did his thing, driving toward the hoop and jumping up with a taller guy all over him. He seemed to hang in the air for a full minute. His legs were splayed and his left elbow (he was a lefty) stuck out like divining rod. And then somehow, some way, he got off a hook shot (it was the only shot available to him) and it banked off the backboard and through the net.

And he came down laughing and turned around and looked at me as if to say, "See? That's how it's done, son."

. . .

And sometimes, it is.

Retired Navy Lt. Cmdr. Joe Langdell died. He was 100 years old, and one of the last witnesses to the Japanese attack on Pearl Harbor on December 7, 1941. My father was also a Lt. Cmdr. in WWII.

So I am saddened when another one of these heroes drops out of our lives. It's like you're getting a chunk of Earth chopped off a hillside. Pretty soon we're not going to have any hills. We are just going to have people sitting on the rubble wondering where bravery and sacrifice have gone.

· · ·

We used to train our young in the virtues of bravery and sacrifice. We don't anymore. And yet these concepts are so hardwired into our souls that it is very likely a clue to what is really going on in the universe. Let me explain.

What is the most famous ending in Hollywood history? It is *Casablanca*. You recall that it is the story of Rick, an American who has opened up a café in French occupied territory during World War II. He has done so, we learn, because he is trying to forget a woman. And what a woman she is, Ilsa Lund. She looks exactly like Ingrid Bergman. Rick was in love with her, and she with him, in Paris. But then Ilsa discovered that her husband, Victor Laszlo, was still alive. He did not die in a concentration camp as she had been told. So she leaves Rick in Paris, without explanation, and he takes that as a betrayal. He has come to Casablanca now to run his saloon and forget her. He wants nothing to do with the war effort. His code is, "I stick my neck out for nobody."

But then one night Ilsa and her husband walk into the café. Rick now has to deal with the old wound. Over the course of the movie it becomes clear that they still love each other, and Ilsa finally agrees to go away with Rick out of Casablanca, via a plane to Lisbon.

But when Rick meets Ilsa at the airport, he tells her he is not going with her, that she needs to get on the plane with her husband. He says there are bigger things than the problems of three small people. Ilsa leaving with Rick would ruin Laszlo and destroy his important work. If she were to go away with Rick she would regret it, maybe not now, but soon and for the rest of her life. As a tear rolls down her cheek, Rick reminds her, "We'll always have Paris."

What Rick is doing is sacrificing the thing he wants most in the world. He is doing it for a greater good. After Ilsa and Victor leave on the plane, Rick is left standing there with the corpse of a Nazi major, whom he has killed, and the French police captain, Louis. It looks like curtains for Mr. Rick Blaine. But when the police arrive, Louis says, "Round up the usual suspects." Then Louis and Rick walk off together, to rejoin the war effort. It is the beginning of a beautiful friendship.

What we have here is a story of sacrifice and resurrection.

Gee, that sounds rather familiar. It is, in fact, the central story of our civilization.

Now why should that be? Perhaps it is wired into us as a receptor, as a clue to what is good and essential in existence. And when we read a story with sacrifice in it, whether it's a true story or fiction, it moves us. It is supposed to move us.

It is interesting to note that four hundred years before Christ, another story of sacrifice was told by the Greek playwright Euripides. It is a play about a queen named Alcestis. She's married to King Admetus, who has an appointment with Death. The king is scheduled to eat a dirt sandwich unless he can find someone willing to take his place. No one volunteers for that duty. So Queen Alcestis steps up to do it. Out of her deep love for her husband, she agrees to go off with Death in his place.

Sacrifice.

Meanwhile, Hercules comes to visit the palace, and the king makes like all is well, and commands his servants to serve Herc plenty of wine, which the big guy is more than happy to imbibe. He gets tipsy, the servants get angry, and finally one of them spills the beans on why Herc's merry-making is so out of place.

Hercules is deeply moved by the story of Alcestis's sacrifice. So he runs out to intercept her from Death. He subdues Death and returns to the palace with a veiled Alcestis. The king doesn't know it's her yet. Herc says he wishes he had the power to bring his wife back and restore the king's joy, but the king says, "The dead shall never rise."

Then Hercules unveils Alcestis and has the king take her hand. The king at first thinks it's just a phantom, but Hercules tells of fighting with Death and bringing Alcestis back. The king is overjoyed and speaks to her, but Hercules tells him she has been among the dead and will not be able to speak for three days.

· · ·

After three days, resurrection. Hmmm...where did Euripides get that bit of inspiration? Why three days? What source of creativity gave that story of sacrifice and new life to a Greek playwright?

It almost seems like that Source was using a play among pagans to prepare them for another death, burial, and resurrection to come when the Romans ran things. The final lines of *The Alcestis* come from the Chorus:

There be many shapes of mystery;
    And many things God brings to be,
    Past hope or fear.
    And the end men looked for cometh not,
    And a path is there where no man thought.
    So hath it fallen here.

A path where we would not expect one. The defeat of Death, the way of new life.

Sacrifice and resurrection are clues. But we are increasingly a society that doesn't look for clues. We're too busy texting, baking, ranting, raging, and making asses of ourselves. We all need some butt kicking by Hercules.

In April, 1917, a puckish, fun loving nineteen-year-old Marine named Frederick Hamilton "Ted" Fox was about to be shipped off to France. His mother, Esther, and sister, Frederica (whom everyone called "Freddy") came to the train station to see him off.

Ted Fox was my great uncle. I am told he had a generous and robust spirit, and a smile that could light up a room. Esther looks so proud of him. And my great aunt Freddy has the most engaging, vivacious and interested look about her. She was an artist, and in those heady days just before the Roaring '20's she had an artist's temperament about living life to the full. They all came together in this amazing photo:

Corporal Ted Fox arrived in France and began preparing for action. It came in June of 1918, in what came to be known as the Battle of Belleau Wood.

At dawn on June 7th, the Marines were ordered to advance toward the German lines and their deadly machine gun nests.

The first wave ended in slaughter.

Ted Fox's squad, along with another, were dispatched to flank the nests. They cleaned out one, and went for another. It was during this second wave that Ted Fox, leading his men, was killed by a bullet to the head.

News traveled slowly in those days, and it took nearly six months for Esther to receive the final news of her son's sacrifice. She'd written a letter to a naval hospital and that letter was seen by a wounded soldier. He took it upon himself to write to her.

Great Lakes, Ill.
  February 15th, 1919

Dear Friend Mrs. Fox- - -

. . .

My attention was called to a letter you wrote the hospital in rela-
tion to your son who was killed in action. He was in the same
company and platoon that I was. I did not see your son fall but I
assure you that he fought gallantly for his country and died upon
the field of battle bravely. I'm sure his last thoughts were of his
dear Mother at home and praying that the news of his death would
not be too great a shock to her. As being in battle I know that one
thinks of his dear ones at home and not of what may happen to
oneself. We all knew that we were either going to be killed or
wounded in such a terrific battle that was then raging but all faced
it bravely and fought fiercely until we fell. I was wounded severely
but escaped with my life in the same battle that your son was
killed . . .

Mrs. Fox, I know that you are and should be very proud to be a
mother of such a son that volunteering gave his life to his country.

All the boys that died on the field of battle will never be forgotten
and shall be honored by their comrades.

A Marine,

Private Roy R. Drowty
  U.S. Naval Hospital
  Great Lakes, Ill.

War is hell. And young men and women, wave after wave of
them, have gone into hell for us. I don't care what side of the

political spectrum you come from. Each of us owe our war dead and wounded all the honor we can bestow. They're not politicians or pundits. They're the brave ones who've been there for us, no matter what we believe. In fact, so that we can continue to believe what we want and talk about it, demonstrate about it, vote on it.

The line in Private Drowty's letter that stands out for me is this one: *We all knew that we were either going to be killed or wounded in such a terrific battle that was then raging but all faced it bravely and fought fiercely until we fell.*

In the last stanza of Lt. Col. John McCrae's World War I poem "In Flanders Fields" (referring to a place where war dead were buried) we, the living, are given a charge:

To you from failing hands we throw

The torch; be yours to hold it high.
    If ye break faith with us who die

We shall not sleep, though poppies grow

In Flanders fields.

∼

Gary Owens died. He was 80. A legendary voice in Southern California radio, Owens went on to some fame as the announcer on *Rowan & Martin's Laugh-In,* a comedy show in the late '60s that opened the door for later TV comedy like *Saturday Night Live.* When I was a kid I used to listen to Owens on KMPC, a station my mom liked for its soft pop music. I listened to Owens for his comedy. He was fast and funny and did bits that made me laugh out loud.

Sometimes it was word play. I remember once he played off the Jerry Lee Lewis song title "Whole Lotta Shakin' Goin' On" when, after playing the theme from the TV show *Mission: Impossible* he said, "There's a whole Lalo Schifrin goin' on."

He made up words, too, like *insegrevious.* It has no real meaning, but sounds like it does. In fact, it can mean two different things. A man could say to his wife, "Honey, that dress makes you look absolutely insegrevious," and mean it makes her look good ... but she could take it as *I look fat.*

Owens was similar to another comedian I loved, Steve Allen. They were both intelligent, enjoyed games with the language, and could make a quip right on the spot. Steve Allen did not make it to 80, but to 78, dying in the year 2000 from a massive heart attack that may have been triggered by a seemingly benign fender-bender. Allen, of course, was the creator of *The Tonight Show,* which was later turned over to Jack Paar and then Johnny Carson.

. . .

So a good part of the way I look at and react to the world was formed by Owens and Allen and other comedy geniuses, which is a good thing, because life needs a lot of comedic refraction or you'll just go around depressed all day. You've got to laugh. You've got to see the absurd as well as the cogent. You've got to be able to give a rip-roaring snort at stupidity, which is on display somewhere every moment. You've got to be able to say, when things in the world are spinning faster and faster out of control, that the whole darn thing is simply and unalterably insegrevious.

Rose E. Frisch died. She was 96. She was a scientist whose claim to fame was the linking of body fat with fertility. She found out that young women with very little body fat, like athletes or anorexics, had trouble getting pregnant. Some women athletes who stopped working out so they could fatten up a bit and have a baby named their daughters Rose in tribute to Ms. Frisch.

That's a nice thing to do, to pay a little homage, a little tribute, to someone who has helped you along the way, even if you have never met that person. We had neighbors once with two boys, and because the father was a sports fanatic they named them after favorite athletes, only they inverted the names. One was named Ryan Nolan, for Nolan Ryan, the great baseball hurler. The other was Taylor Lawrence, for Lawrence Taylor, the feared linebacker for the New York Giants, a Hall of Famer, but whose life has been riddled with drug use and sexual misconduct, which means you need to be very careful about naming your children after star athletes at the height of their powers, for there is risk involved. I wonder how many children named O.J. had to change their names later in life. I think there might not be too great a risk in naming your child Tebow Timothy, but there might be if you named him Manziel Johnny. First of all, everyone would call him Manny. Second of all, the jury is still out on whether Johnny Manziel is going to turn out to be a star or a bust in the NFL. As I write this he is in rehab for his excess drinking and a party life-style, which hampered his preparations for actual games, which, when he finally got into them, created a fog of stink around the field. So hold off on naming your son Manziel Johnny and wait a few seasons to see how things turn out.

Michael D. Briscoe died at the age of 57. Very few people, relatively speaking, know his name. His obit in the *Louisville Courier-Journal* states only that he was a retired Heavy Equipment Operator for Abel Construction Company and a member of the Laborers and Operators Unions. In other words, the quintessential American working man, operating those big cats for this company that was, I discovered upon further investigation, founded by a former professional boxer in 1938. It is a company that is based in Kentucky, and there is a quintessential American state for you, it even sounds good in the back of the throat. Ken TUCK Eee. It's the land that old Daniel Boone settled in before America was even a country, back when it was still colonies under the thumb of England. Daniel Boone became a legendary frontiersman, and in the 1960s was immortalized in a television show starring Fess Parker as Boone, wearing a coonskin cap which Parker had made famous in the 1950s playing Davy Crockett for Walt Disney, and becoming a national icon.

Fess Parker was a smart man, and while he was at the height of his popularity he bought a lot of land in Santa Barbara and beyond, and became wealthy because of it, and started a winery called, to no one's great shock, Fess Parker Winery, which has gone on to produce many very fine and award-winning wines.

Wine, we now know, is good for us, when taken in moderation. That's why the first miracle in the New Testament is Jesus turning water into wine—the *best* wine according to the banquet master—and doing it for a party. Thus, contrary to what some teetotalers may think, it may actually be sacrilegious *not* to drink wine, for it is good for your heart (see Psalm 104:15) and we are to treat our bodies like temples, and temples without good hearts are not going to be around as long. So the wisdom of the poet stands:

God, in his goodness, gave us the grape
  To cheer both great and small.
  Little fools will drink too much,
  Great fools none at all.

But how much is too much is a matter of experience and bodily makeup. Which takes me back to Flagstaff, Arizona. I was with my high school church group, taking a week in the summer to do volunteer work for the Hopi. Our bus had stopped for the night and we brought our sleeping bags and duffels into the fellowship hall of a local church. We were told by our adult leaders to relax, read, play games, listen to the radio—but by all means stay inside the hall! Which of course my friend Randy and I interpreted as meaning: "Feel free to wander into town and find some trouble to get into."

· · ·

Ever ready to follow instructions as we understood them, Randy and I slipped out the side doors and started a nocturnal tour of the bustling Flagstaff metropolis, which seemed to have, as they used to say, rolled up the sidewalks.

So we walked and talked and came to a railroad crossing, moving therefrom into the soft red-and-yellow neon of a LIQUOR STORE sign. To a couple of seventeen-year-olds on a nighttime prowl, such illumination is catnip. Randy suggested we baptize our adventure with a bottle.

I agreed, as Randy Winter was my brother from another mother, my closest friend, with whom I laughed much and talked deeply. We would discuss with equal fervor the mystery of girls and the character of God (whose reputation, by the way, we were failing to uphold as we schemed how to lay our hands on some demon intoxicant).

Our first order of business was what manner of spirits to acquire. As an athlete who was not a member of the party circuit, I was not an imbiber of any sort. I did not like the taste of beer. I'd snuck a nip of gin once in my parents' liquor cabinet and wondered why on earth anyone would want to drink gasoline.

So Randy suggested we try some wine. He'd heard that Boone's Farm Apple Wine went down nicely, and the decision was made.

· · ·

Then the next step: to lurk in the shadows of the parking lot until a car drove up, then casually approach the driver with a request that he be our procurer. This was nervous time, for who knew what kind of personality we would engage? What if it was an off-duty cop? Or some old Veteran of Foreign Wars who'd want to lecture us on the evils of drink?

A chance we would have to take. Which we did presently when a car drove in, and out stepped a man of about thirty, with long hair. Long hair! A good sign. A hippie perhaps, or at least a musician. In either case, cool. We emerged from our hiding spot and said, "Excuse me ..."

The man stopped and read our faces in the soft, primrose light. "You want me to get you a bottle, don't you?" he said.

We nodded. My face felt flush, as if the entire world were witnessing my iniquity.

The man laughed. "I used to do the same thing. What do you want?"

We gave the man a couple of fins, our pooled resources, and Randy said, "Boone's Farm Apple Wine."

It seemed to me the man hesitated, as if to give us one last chance to reconsider our fate. And then he went through the door.

. . .

Randy and I high-fived our success. And soon thereafter we had in our hands a brown paper bag and some change, passed to us with a "Good luck" sentiment from our partner in crime.

We left the scene of our misdemeanor, went back near the railroad tracks, and sat cross-legged on the ground.

Randy unscrewed the top. We were too unsophisticated to smell the cap.

Then he drank and passed the bottle to me. I took a tentative sip. Ah, I thought. *Sprightly, with a conversational fruitiness and subdued notes of summer.* (Actually, what I really thought was, *This isn't so bad.*)

And so 'neath the Arizona stars Randy Winter and I shared a bottle of what was generously classified as wine, and discovered something interesting about the human body, namely, that there is a lag time between the ingestion of alcoholic content and its effect on one's physiology.

Which meant, at one point, it suddenly felt as if a switch was flipped in my brain. The disco ball lit up and went round and round, and I heard myself say something like, "Rammy, my headth pinning" before I teetered backward and ended up on the gravel, looking up at the stars as they raced around the heavens like sparkling emergency room nurses shouting, "Stat! Stat!"

Which is the last thing I remember about that night. In the morning I was in my sleeping bag on the church floor. At least I think it was my sleeping bag. My stomach felt like a balloon of toxic gasses. Two miniature railroad workers were on either side of my head, driving spikes into my temples with their sledge-hammers.

The adult leaders were none too pleased with Randy and me. We knew we'd messed up, crossed the line, failed to represent our church. We were threatened with expulsion, which would mean a long and humiliating drive for our parents to come pick us up. We threw ourselves upon the mercy of the court and were granted a temporary stay. I began then to truly appreciate the power of forgiveness. Plus, I was ready to swear off booze for good.

Honest, hard work kept Randy and me on the straight and narrow for at least a week. There's a victory in there somewhere.

Randy died at the age of nineteen. Leukemia. When I think about him, and all the good times we had, this particular memory is the one that surfaces first.

Why is that? Maybe because it typified our friendship. We took risks together, got in trouble on occasion, but mostly laughed. A couple of times there were tears. There's something deeply meaningful to me in all this, and if I explore it I sense it will tell me something about what I write and why. It may also be a story idea trying to get out.

Early in his career Ray Bradbury started making lists of nouns, many of them based on childhood memories. Things like *The Lake, The Night, The Crickets, The Ravine.*

"These lists were the provocations," he writes in Zen in the Art of Writing, "that caused my better stuff to surface. I was feeling my way toward something honest, hidden under the trapdoor on the top of my skull."

The "trapdoor material" will teach you, too, if you're open. For I don't believe I've had a taste of Boone's Farm wine since that night. Nothing against it, you understand, but I prefer a nice California cab. I'm sure Randy Winter, my best friend, would approve.

Louis Jourdan, described by the *L.A. Times* as a "dashing Frenchman," died. He was 93, which is another shocker because, like most Frenchmen of that era, he smoked like a proverbial chimney. Yet there he was, right up there into 2015, still alive, mostly forgotten, which is the tale of this world, as old Marcus Aurelius said 1,860 years ago, that you have to realize as soon as you're gone, as soon as time goes by, you're not going to be remembered by very many people, and even now how many people know who Marcus Aurelius was? How many people have actually read his *Meditations*? Maybe he's the answer to a question on the SAT or in a trivia game, but that still slices down considerably the number of people who are familiar with this Roman emperor who wrote some of the best stuff in history about who we are and how we should think about who we are.

. . .

So there was Louis Jourdan, a big heartthrob to moviegoers when he starred in the musical *Gigi* with Leslie Caron and Maurice Chevalier. That got him a few good roles for a few years, but then as happens with any throb, he gets a bit older and the roles change, and he went from romantic leading man to villain in one of the James Bond movies, a role perfect for a dashing Frenchman because all great Bond villains have an accent of some kind. What is it about accents that make villains more sinister? I suppose it's the notion of being set apart, of not being American and therefore not playing by the rules, although Eric Bogosian played a pretty good villain in the Steven Seagal movie *Under Siege 2: Dark Territory,* in which Bogosian is a computer nerd turned terrorist and has about the most American accent you can find even in an American movie. It was a pretty good flick, too, probably the high point of Seagal's career, and there is another example of how things change the older you get, for Seagal became a king of direct-to-video stuff, which is sort of like how Nick Nolte became a king of sorts in the John Milius movie, *Farewell to the King,* ruling over a small tribe in Borneo. And there's another example, Nick Nolte that is, of things changing over time, because at some point Nick Nolte went from having a normal voice to having a voice that sounded like a cement mixer full of radio parts, and then there was that DUI bust and perhaps the worst mug shot in law enforcement history.

Although the shirt was nice.

So we were talking about Louis Jourdan, and how many people today would even know his name, especially Millennials, who think a classic film is *E.T.* and who will look at you when you say, "Louis Jourdan," and say, "Oh yeah, isn't he a clothes designer or something?"

And so you do your work and you have your day, and that's all you can do, the rest is up to history and time and no one is much remembered after they die, except among the immediate family, and then when the immediate family goes the memory gets a little fuzzier, unless there is a solid reason for the family to keep remembering. Which reminds me of a little joke about spinning the family legacy. It goes like this:

. . .

The Smiths were proud of their family tradition. Their ancestors had come to America on the *Mayflower*. Their relatives included senators and Wall Street wizards.

They decided to compile a family history, a legacy for their children and grandchildren, and hired a fine author. Only one problem arose: how to handle the black sheep of the family, George, who was executed in the electric chair at the state prison, for murder.

The author assured them he could handle the story tactfully.

When the book appeared, the entry on George said this: "Great-uncle George occupied a chair of applied electronics at an important government institution. He was attached to his position by the strongest of ties, and his death came as a great shock."

You can only control so much of what people say about you, so live your life in the present day, each day, doing what good you can, taking care of your business. And try not to get taken in for a mug shot.

~

Leslie Gore died. She was 68. A teen-age singing idol in the 1960s, she sang about teenie bopper heartbreak, like in the song "It's My Party" which has the lyric, "It's my party and I'll cry if I want to, cry if I want to, cry if I want to," which is how a lot of high school girls felt in those days, when boyfriends or would-be boyfriends would burst the bubble of the girl who was counting on going steady or even getting married—a quaint notion, young people actually wanting to get married and live a family life! So this song of Leslie Gore's told the sad tale of a girl who was hooked on Johnny, but Johnny is seen walking out of her party with Judy, and they're holding hands! So the girl is going to cry, dammit (the word *dammit* is not in the original lyrics, but clearly that's what she's thinking) and she tells people, go ahead, play some more records, but I'm not going to pretend I'm happy till Johnny gets his butt back in here (the word *butt* is not in the lyrics) and starts treating me right again, not running outside with that tart Judy (no *tart,* either) and then, at the end of the song, here they are, Johnny and Judy, and they're coming back into the party, but guess what? Judy is wearing Johnny's ring! That's where the song ends, but it could have continued, "It's my party, and I'll throw the record player at Johnny if I want to, record player at Johnny if I want to, record player at Johnny if I want to."

So there it was, an anthem to the heartache felt by a million girls on the cusp of the sexual revolution of the 1960s, and maybe it was Leslie Gore's song that led to the burgeoning feminist movement, where doggone it, they weren't going to take that from Johnny anymore, and not only that, they were going to demand to be treated fairly by Johnny's father who ran the office where they worked.

So it wasn't an accident that shortly after "It's My Party" Leslie Gore had another hit called "You Don't Own Me," and it was definitely a tell-off song to Johnny and his ilk, the song telling him, I'm not one of your toys, okay? So don't put me on display, and quit telling me what to say and do all the time. I'm young and free, and I like it that way, and if you don't want another record player thrown at your head, just quit acting like you own me, fella.

And the song was picked up as a feminist anthem and Leslie Gore did not rest on her teen-age singer laurels, but went to Sarah Lawrence College and graduated with a degree in English, and good for her. Parties are fine, but education is better, a lesson lost today, especially in those places where weed is legal and ambition and study habits have died like wounded soldiers left behind on the cultural battlefield.

It is ironic, isn't it, that God gave man dominion over the plants, and now in two states (with more to come) a plant is exercising dominion over man. Fire me up, dude.

Tiger Woods' golf game died. It was around 37 years old, as the young Eldrick "Tiger" Woods started playing the game when he was two, at the urging of his pop. It was a painful death to watch, as the formerly unbeatable Mr. Woods became not just a journeyman player, but one of the worst players on the tour, missing cuts and looking like a weekend duffer with a couple of beers in him. The jury is still out on whether this death will be permanent, or if there will be a resurrection, but with each passing month, and with injuries plaguing him, it looks as if his game is a cold stiff. And it all seems traceable not to his lower body, but to the area between his ears, his mental state, which, as

I noted in the first selection in this book, came about when his lovely wife, Elin, heard a Tiger voicemail that went like this: "Hey, it's, uh … it's Tiger. Can you please take your name off your phone? My wife went through my phone and, uh, may be calling you, so if you can, please take your name off that. And, um … just have it as a number on the voice mail. OK? You got to do this for me. Huge. Quickly. All right, bye." And then it was all over, everyone knew, and the tightly controlled Tiger world, which he'd managed with a group of acolytes for over ten years, was kaput. The decline started then, and it was all in his head, and once it gets into your head, if you're a golfer, it's very hard to ever get it out. Just ask a golfer named David Duval, who was once #1 in the world, and who shot a 59 one time, which has only been done half a dozen times in the whole history of golf, and then boom, one day the game left David Duval and he couldn't get it back, he dropped down, down, down and his head betrayed his body and there was just nothing he could do. All professional golfers fear this, which is why there is an industry known as "sports psychology" where you hire a Ph.D to keep you thinking good thoughts.

But good thoughts are not coming to Tiger Woods, though he puts a good face on it all, and smiles for the cameras, and says things are "coming along" even though they are clearly not, and what will happen? Will he keep trying or retire? If he does retire, he'll never get to the magic goal he's always had—to surpass Mr. Jack Nicklaus on the major championships list. Tiger has won fourteen majors. Jack won eighteen. That's four big ones Tiger has to win, and it's not looking good, because Tiger Woods himself brought on the great golf revival, and all these seven- eight- nine-year olds who watched the young Tiger winning went out and took up the game and now they are on the tour playing better golf than any generation before, and Tiger is among the older generation, and he just doesn't intimidate the kids anymore.

Not only that, but Woods left at least half-a-dozen major championships out there by messing with his swing. He was dominant, fearsome, unbeatable, and then he fired his swing coach, the hugely successful Butch Harmon, to try to remake his swing in some other guy's image, and he just didn't win like he used to. Then he changed swings again, and it's all a mess now, the lesson being this: if you are married to a lovely woman who is a good wife and mother, don't go drilling for oil in foreign fields, don't be a liar and a cheater and expect that it won't affect your personal life and then your professional life. Don't think you can escape cosmic justice, even if you have a cool name like Tiger.

Sam Andrew died at the age of 73, which is a pretty good run considering he was right in the middle of the eye of the storm in the time that was defined by sex, drugs, and rock 'n roll, for you could not get any closer, any more involved, any more vortexed, than to be the guy playing guitar next to Janis Joplin, who was the voice, the queen, the poster child of that era—extreme, burned out, dead of an overdose—and Sam Andrew was there, was guitar player for, and lover of, Janis, and somehow he came out of that and made it past the big 7-Oh. Sam Andrew founded a band called Big Brother and the Holding Company, playing psychedelic music, as it was called back then, in and around San Francisco, and in 1966 the band's manager brought in this girl from Texas to sing for them, and it was Janis, and because Big Brother played real loud, Janis had to scream her songs, and that became her signature, and the band and Janis blew away the rock world for a couple of years, until Janis left to go solo and Sam Andrew went with her. And that's when things got very '6os, for they started shooting heroin together, then Janis fired him from her band, then they became lovers, and there was no rhyme or reason, which is how rock and roll is summed up in the movie *School of Rock*, where Jack Black plays a wannabe rocker fired from his own startup band and scores a job as a teacher in an elite school, but really only knows music, and helps the kids express themselves through rock and roll, and one of the kids comes up with a song for his teacher, one of the lines being, "Rock got no reason, rock got no rhyme," and then, ironically, the next line rhymes: "You bettah get me to school on time," which just goes to show that rock is a wild jungle of a place, where you can shoot horse and get fired and still end up in the bed of the rock goddess who told you to hit the road.

So Sam Andrew survived, Janis did not, and that's the story, or a big part of the story, for getting through life. It is a lot like survival, and some make it, and some don't. Some good people get cut down too early, and some bad people not soon enough, and down here it seems like dice, but up there it is seen as a world where we're given free will, we are not robots or chairs or olives, but people with souls and wills who can do bad things, or good things, can choose to love our neighbor or be a permanent putz, but to all the PPs out there, there's going to be a day of reckoning.

Which reminds me again of Steve Allen, whom I've mentioned, the comic genius. One of his bits from an old TV show was an Old West set, and it was like the beginning of a movie, and two cowboys meet at a fence, and the conversation goes something like this:

. . .

"Reckon there's gonna be trouble in town today."
   "I reckon you're right."
   "You reckon we need to strap on our guns?"
   "I reckon so!"

Then the title of the movie flashes across the screen: DAY OF RECKONING.

Movita died. She was 98. Movita was her movie star name, her full name being Movita Castaneda. She was a Mexican beauty who had the misfortune to marry Marlon Brando, a man for whom marriage was not designed, and he proved it by cheating on his wife with a young Polynesian actress named Tarita on the set of the 1962 film *Mutiny on the Bounty*. When Movita unsurprisingly broke up with Brando, he showed his lack of class by taking from the mother of his two children her nice Mercedes and giving her instead an old station wagon. Movita was reduced to working for a Santa Monica auto shop, delivering car batteries to customers.

Which only goes to show, once again, that the most talented among us may also be the most loathsome, and it's too bad for Brando, because he is in my opinion the finest actor our country has ever produced—Spencer Tracy is a close second—and he was given practically god status in the 1950s, which can't be good for a young man's psyche, and it wasn't good for Brando, who became fat and weird in his later years, stopping back on Earth every now and then for a performance that reminded us of just how great he was, like in *The Godfather* and *The Freshman* (where he does a hilarious send up of his Don Corleone role).

Don't let anyone turn you into a god. It's not good for you.

Be like Jimmy Stewart instead. A tall, lanky lad becomes an improbable movie star, wins an Oscar, goes off to fly bombers in World War II, comes home and makes a legendary movie, *It's A Wonderful Life,* gets married and stays married to the same woman, attends church on Sunday, changes his "brand" by going into Westerns, and becomes iconic there, too, and never puts on airs or treats people like dung.

That's a good life, yes, a wonderful life. Sorry for Movita that she got mixed up with the wrong guy.

June Fairchild died. She was 68. Her obituary said she was an actress who ended up living on Skid Row. I didn't know her name, but apparently she was in some movies in the '70s, including *Thunderbolt and Lightfoot* starring Clint Eastwood and Jeff Bridges. But she lost her career to drugs and alcohol, and lived a street existence where women fall prey to robbery and rape.

I'm familiar with Skid Row in downtown Los Angeles, having grown up in this town but also doing some in-depth research for my novel *Try Darkness*, and getting a ride-along with an LAPD detective who pointed out the various types who live in this block area of our city. Some of the denizens knew him and waved and shouted his name, which was an odd feeling, like being on a Rose Parade float with the grand marshal. In any event, the question of how to deal with drug addicts and the poor plagues us and there is no single answer that will satisfy everyone. It is up to individuals to do what they can. My church regularly goes downtown with blankets and food to help alleviate some of the suffering, but a large scale solution raises questions about the role of government and business and people and capitalism and socialism and everybody has an opinion, and virtually nobody wants to listen to contrary views.

Which is a thing now, the not listening. People have the idea that they are entitled to their own opinion. That's actually not true. They are entitled to *express* their own opinion, but in order to hold an *actual* opinion you have to be able to back it up, offer evidence, use logic and facts, but this very practice is not taught in our schools anymore, because it's all about feelings. So if I have a feeling that I have an opinion, I can feel it loudly on a talk show, or when I am confronted with a better argument, I can ignore the evidence and not change my mind, simply stating, Well, that's only *your* opinion. But instead of offering a reason that one opinion is better than another, we run around thinking all opinions are equally valid, and then we become a giant henhouse of cackling fowl.

～

Harris Wittels died. He was only 30, and died of an overdose of drugs. Tragic, always, and young Harris was a comedian, producer, and writer for a hit comedy called *Parks and Recreation*, and no one knows what inner demons drove him to seek solace in drugs, but it's an old story for creative people, isn't it? Creatives cannot stand days where they think about cheese or chairs. They have to think about lots of things at once, and sometimes that can be an actual burden, as it was for Robin Williams, who had just about the most fertile and dizzying comic mind of all time, jumping from one thing to the next like a sand flea hopping oily bodies on Santa Monica beach. The question arises, did that synaptic brilliance cause chemical anomalies that affected Robin's brain? Who knows? It's a mystery, except that creatives, especially comedians, have been known to dwell in darkness even as they try to lighten everybody else's day.

Hemingway was probably bipolar and dealt with it through bravado and vodka, and then they fried his brain with electroshock, and then he lost his ability to write, and that was the one thing he just could not lose, it wasn't like an ex-wife, of which he had several, it was the very thing that defined him, and with that gone he put a shotgun to his head and blasted. The year was 1961.

Hunter S. Thompson also died of a self-inflicted gunshot, in 2005, though he might have been a singular case, for that man was a laboratory of drug use, he should have died long ago of all the chemicals he put into his body, chased by hearty doses of Wild Turkey, and still, through it all, the man could write and entertain, mainly in the pages of *Rolling Stone*, but also in a book called *Fear and Loathing in Las Vegas,* which has the legendary opening line: *We were somewhere around Barstow on the edge of the desert when the drugs began to take hold.*

. . .

He also wrote, "Every now and then when your life gets complicated and the weasels start closing in, the only cure is to load up
on heinous chemicals and then drive like a bastard from Hollywood to Las Vegas." Which is not really a cure, nor a thing
anyone should ever do, but captures the mind of the crazy and
creative Thompson, and just a little of what it means to be a
writer, because writers have to go a bit crazy when they write, not
the bad drug-induced crazy, but the kind of crazy Ray Bradbury
was, getting up each morning and stepping on a land mine (so he
said), the land mine being him, and after he exploded on the
page, only then pick up the pieces and see what he had. But in
that land mine phase, that's the place where creativity happens,
and as long as you make that your only drug (not counting
Flonase® or Nyquil® or what your doctor orders) then it's good to
let that be your high for the day, and not try to find it or calm it or
forget it in a bottle or a needle or a pipe.

It is sad that we won't get more comedy from Harris Wittels,
because he had a lot of comedy years left. Which is the exact
opposite of what has happened with Bill Cosby, for his comedy
was my favorite for fifty years, since I was a kid, and then came
the accusations of serially drugging and raping young women,
and if it had been only one accuser maybe you could wait for the
trial, but it was so many with no other motive than to tell the
truth, and who at the time feared they would not be believed, and
so now we have the comedy of Bill Cosby dying at the last stage
of his career, for how can we laugh anymore at what this man
says or does? And all the classic routines—from Noah to Fat
Albert—gone, burned up, only a memory now.

. . .

Please, no more death to comedy, we need as much of it as we can get these days just to stay sane.

Yutaka Katayama died. He was a remarkable 105. He was also an auto executive, for Datsun, and came up with the Datsun 240 Z, a legendary automobile that survived the takeover by Nissan. My good friend Charles has a silver Z, and he loves the speed, though not the gas mileage. Katayama was inducted into the U.S. Automotive Hall of Fame, and also the Tokyo Hall of Fame, which is two halls of fame, and I didn't even know they had them for auto executives, but why not? And congratulations to him, posthumously, for making it.

At one time, when I was a kid, my dream was to someday make the Baseball Hall of Fame. I was an okay Little League baseball player, but not quite the All Star I wanted to be. My sport turned out to be basketball. My basketball idol was Bill Bradley, because I read a book about him called *A Sense of Where You Are* about his basketball career at Princeton. He was the best player in the land his senior year, but he didn't go pro, he went to Oxford as a Rhodes Scholar, and after two years came back and joined the New York Knicks and helped them win two championships. Then he went to the United States Senate and then he ran for president as a Democrat, but lost in the primaries to Al Gore, and it was a real contest for which one of these two was the dullest speaker. It is a golden tongue now that carries the day, as long as you have a good-looking pan (*pan* is a word from the 1920s that means *face*) and an electorate as ignorant as ours has become, who like golden tongues and nice pans.

Agnes Stevens died. She was 79 and a former nun and school-teacher who started a program called "School on Wheels" to help poor kids in Southern California stay in school. She got a bunch of volunteers to become tutors and they would roll up to where the impoverished kids were and teach them, give them backpacks, and keep them interested in learning, which is something every kid deserves. Agnes Stevens was one of those ordinary citizens who sees a problem and finds a way to solve it, showing that we have "better angels" in our natures and the trick in our communal lives is figuring out ways to coax those better angels out to be in command and control, but that's a very hard thing to do without home and school and faith community working together, which is getting harder and harder as homes bust up and school boards go batty with the "latest ideas." Some ideas, no matter how late, are still batty.

That's really the balancing act, knowing when to try something and when not to, when to experiment and when to use what's tried and true, and even more, when to take that experiment wide, make it what's called a "social experiment," the problem being that you have to have lab mice, and when those lab mice are kids in school you're talking about a lifetime of effects. So there are two kinds of people in the social sciences, as it were, the kind who want to keep trying new things and the kind who say, Hold on there, what we've been doing has worked pretty well, do you really want to mess it all up?

You have to have both sides going at it to make progress and also keep from blowing yourself up, and your society, too, and that used to be called the Rhythm of Life, you needed to love experiment and change, but also needed to love and honor the permanent things that are worth preserving. The best creative experimentation is done by artists, and you have the same voices, the ones who want to be new and different and the ones who want to use the forms that have worked over time, and the perfect subject of the former view is Jackson Pollock, an artist who threw paint on canvas and people went gaga over it, but if you don't tell people who did it they'd look at it and say, *What happened to that poor canvas?*

So Jackson Pollock is on one end of the creative scale, and on the other you have Barbara Cartland, who wrote romances by formula and became one of the most prolific authors in the world. She did not look like Jackson Pollock. She wore loud and ostentatious makeup and furs, but most of all she wrote like a piston engine, and produced well over 700 books in her lifetime, though most of those books were pretty slim romances, so it would take about ten Cartlands to equal one Tolstoy. She died at the age of 98, but in her younger years she was apparently naïve about matters sexual, for a dashing soldier in the British Army fell for her and proposed and she accepted, then went home and told her mother. Her mother, with great reluctance but a sense of parental duty, sat young Barbara down and explained to her the "facts of life," at which the young Barbara recoiled. She broke off the engagement, causing the young soldier to threaten to shoot himself outside a popular café. He did not, and his actions no doubt shaped Barbara Cartland's view of the male love interest in her novels, as perhaps did another dashing soldier who asked Barbara to come up to his room so he could show her "how my revolver works." She refused him as well.

· · ·

Perhaps Barbara Cartland looked back on her mother as a valued teacher, like Agnes Stevens must have been, though in a rather more personal capacity. We need all kinds of education, but in the proper venue, thanks.

Betty Buchel died. She was 85, and all it says in her obit is that she was "a wonderful and extremely thoughtful person with an extraordinary sense of humor" and if one line is all you get, that seems to me to be one that can hardly be improved upon. The breed of human being we call "thoughtful" is in danger of extinction, the kind of person who does things for others without expecting anything in return. The kind of person who remembers your birthday when they don't really have any need to, or who hears you are sick and shows up at your door with a Tupperware full of chicken soup from an old family recipe.

But then you add to that, like real whipped cream on top of the chocolate shake, an extraordinary sense of humor. It's quite lovely to find someone with any sense of humor at all, but an extraordinary one is a delight beyond measure A thoughtful person who can make you laugh, that's the kind you want to be around.

I don't know if you can develop a sense of humor or if you have to be born with one. I know some people who cannot tell a joke to save their lives—or, if their lives were truly in danger unless they made someone laugh (the subject matter of a short story of mine called "No Laughing Matter") then I suppose most could at least *tell* a joke, as in mouthing the words, like Benedict Cumberbatch tries to do in *The Imitation Game*, that endearing moment when Alan Turing is trying to get people to like him, but I mean the ability to spin a joke and have people hang on it right up to the punch line.

It is said that the Irish have that in their blood, and my family has Scots-Irish blood running through it, and my father and uncle and grandfather were all great storytellers, and maybe I've got a bit of that in me, too, and I've been told I tell a good joke, but did I study the matter?

I've studied humor and read Steve Allen's book *How to Be Funny*, which is about as straight-on a title as you're going to find on the matter of a sense of humor, but I do think you have to bathe your mind in comedy and practice it to get any good at it. Groucho Marx grew up in a house of Jewish boys all vying for attention from their funny mother, Minnie, so all day long they were playing word games and trying to be faster than each other. So by the time Groucho went from movies to TV, on a show called *You Bet Your Life*, where his main thing was to chat with guests and say funny things based on what the guests told him, he was prepared for it because his whole life had been a preparation for such a gig. There is an infamous cigar quip attributed to Groucho (you can google "cigar" and "You Bet Your Life" to find it), but there's no actual proof he ever said it. A guy named Kermit Schafer put out vinyl records that purported to be actual bloopers from live TV and radio. There was one of "Groucho" making this supposed quip, but clearly the guy on the recording is not Groucho, but a bad Groucho impersonator, of which there have been many.

. . .

I imagine Betty Buchel was humorously dexterous, too, but not bawdy, for she was also thoughtful and thoughtful people don't embarrass other people. Groucho Marx, and his brother Chico, were not so concerned with sparing others' feelings, in fact they liked to skewer them, as Groucho does to the large actress Margaret Dumont in so many of his movies, like when he is proposing marriage to her and says, "I can see you bending over a hot stove. But I can't see the stove."

In point of fact, we laugh harder when there is someone identifiable as the butt of the joke, except when the joke falls flat or is in bad taste, like the joke that splatted at the 2015 Oscar ceremony. Sean Penn, the actor, was announcing the big award, the Best Picture, and the protocol is simply to open the envelope and say, "And the Oscar goes to ..." But Sean Penn decided to make the moment about himself—this is called narcissism—and he said, in reference to the man who directed the soon to be announced best picture, Mr. Alejandro Inarritu, of Mexico, "Who gave this son of a bitch his green card?" It was supposed to be a hip, satirical send-up, but this child-man came off only as artificial hip, and you could almost hear the voices around the world going, "Did he just say that?"

If you are going to have an extraordinary sense of humor you have to know when *not* to say something as well as when to, and you have to know what moments are appropriate for a laugh. We must teach this to all narcissists, who by definition won't listen, so then we must simply tune them out.

∾

Robert Blees died at the age of 96, a good life for a screenwriter, for that is what Bob Blees was, and with the most amazing
bookend of credits in the history of cinema. On one end, toward
the beginning, is his screenplay for *Magnificent Obsession* starring Jane Wyman and Rock Hudson, and directed by the colorful
Douglas Sirk—and by colorful I mean his use of deep, rich, almost
gaudy colors for his big-screen tear jerkers, of which *Magnificent
Obsession* may be his best, based on the novel by Lloyd Douglas,
but brought to big screen life by Blees (though it was made once
before, in 1935, starring the great Irene Dunne and the almost
great but at least impossibly-good-looking-in-the-1930s Robert
Taylor, who got more rugged in the '40s and '50s and adapted
that image, with a nice deep voice, and many starring roles). Rock
plays a rich playboy who is messing around in a speedboat at
Lake Arrowhead and gets in an accident that requires a "resuscitator," and the only one on the lake belongs to a doctor, who lets it
go to save Rock, but then suffers a heart attack (bad timing) and
since the resuscitator is not with him, he dies. This gets everybody at the local hospital ticked off at Rock, who feels bad
enough to want to buy some forgiveness from the doctor's widow,
played by Jane Wyman. She rebuffs this clod, but he persists, and
he practically stalks her, and she tries to get away from him and
steps right into the path of an oncoming car. She doesn't die, but
she's rendered blind.

Are you with the plot so far? It's got just about everything, doesn't
it? And Blees plays it for all it's worth, and I won't tell you about
what happens after that so you can see the movie for yourself, but
let it be known that in the movie theaters of the 1950s, when this
film was shown, there was not a dry eye in the house, as they used
to say.

· · ·

So that was Blees at the beginning. At the end he was the screen-writer for a movie called *Frogs,* and you cannot get further away from *Magnificent Obsession* than *Frogs,* not even if you had a space shuttle and took off for Uranus. *Frogs* (1972) was a late Ray Milland and early Sam Elliott film, which has become something of a cult classic. It's about an island-dwelling and polluting-the-environment plantation owner (Milland) whose chemicals are causing all sorts of bad things to happen to the flora and fauna, including man-eating tarantulas and voracious, flesh-eating frogs. It was the first flick of its kind, inventing the nature-strikes-back genre. In the end, Sam Elliott has to save the day, and he has the deep voice to do it.

So there was Blees, at either end of a spectrum unlike just about any in Hollywood history, with nice credits in between, including Alfred Hitchcock's TV show and the like.

But the best thing is that Blees was another of the Greatest Generation. He was a bomber navigator for the Army Air Corps in World War II, and as historians will tell you, that was not a job with the best odds of survival. But survive he did, and he wrote, and that's what I would like to do—get to the age of 96, still writing.

Like Herman Wouk, one of the great storytellers of the 20th century, author of *The Caine Mutiny* (Pulitzer Prize winner) and *The Winds of War* and a novel about a novelist, *Youngblood Hawke,* and many more. So there he was in 2012 at the age of 97 with a new book published, *The Law Giver.*

. . .

Not only that! *Booklist* gave it a starred review, and no less than Mr. Stephen King said, *"The Lawgiver* is an unadulterated delight, a compelling, old-fashioned story in sleek new-fashioned clothes. How fortunate it is for readers that Mr. Wouk, who published *The Caine Mutiny* when I was but four years old, has not lost an iota of his storytelling genius. *The Lawgiver* is fast, funny, romantic, and moving."

Can a writer hope for any better way to bid goodbye to his professional world? But I understand Wouk, now 100, is not finished yet. Bravo, Herman! Do not go gentle into that good night or onto that good page!

Donald Keough died. He was 88, and was for a time the #2 man at Coca-Cola during an era called the "soda wars." His job was to beat back the challenge of Pepsi, which was winning the younger set while Coke was out there trying to teach the world to sing in perfect harmony.

He was also the mastermind of one of the worst product blunders in history, which he then turned around into a big bonanza, prompting cynics to suggest his original blunder was not a blunder at all, but a brilliant marketing move. He always denied that, so it was probably a real boner, as they used to say when Fred Merkle was playing baseball.

What Keough did was break something that wasn't broken. The original formula Coke (at least the one that came after they took cocaine out of it) was, and is, the best tasting cola ever. It was Fred Astaire to Pepsi's journeyman hoofer. It was Spencer Tracy to Pepsi's high school senior starring in the school production of *Our Town*.

But for some unknown reason—probably due to overpaid consultants—Keough decided to change the formula, and New Coke was born. With great fanfare they rolled it out. And the country responded with a loud, collective YECCH.

So passionate was the push back that only ten weeks later they brought the old formula back, calling it "Classic Coke."

And sales boomed.

That's the value of free publicity, because the New Coke debacle was written about far and wide.

This is why some people say, "I don't care what you print about me, just spell my name right."

Jerry Lambert died. He was a 74-year-old former jockey. His most famous mount was Native Diver, a Hall of Fame horse, so there is another Hall of Fame they have, which you cannot get in unless you are equine. Jerry Lambert was a small man, because that's what jockeys are. I found this out when I was about eight years old. I liked horses and I had watched an old movie about Seabiscuit, and there was a show on TV called *National Velvet*

which was based on the movie with Elizabeth Taylor which was based on a book.

So I told my mother one day that I wanted to be a jockey. She looked at me and told me I was going to be too big to be a jockey. I was already sprouting. I thought that was a little unfair, this was America and you were supposed to be whatever you wanted to be. But I asked around and sure enough, jockeys are short. My dad even took me to the racetrack at Hollywood Park once, and I got a look at some jockeys and I was already taller than they were. That ended my horse racing career.

The tallest person I ever stood next to was Wilt Chamberlain. This was when I was living in New York, pursuing my acting dream, and I was down in Greenwich Village for some reason, and out on the street was Wilt Chamberlain, which was odd because he so rarely took time away from bedding women, at least according to his boast. So I walked by him and looked up and said, "Hey, Wilt."

He nodded.

My favorite basketball player was Jerry West of the Los Angeles Lakers. They called him Mr. Clutch because he had a way of coming through when it was most needed. The other player I like from those early Laker days was Gail Goodrich, a boy from the San Fernando Valley who was not very tall, but had long arms and was just an all-around great player. It was sort of magical how he did it among all the redwoods he had to play against.

. . .

I love it when people who other people say can't make it in something, because they're too short or too slow or not smart enough or talented enough, I like when those people show the other people how wrong they are, like the NFL teams that passed on drafting Tom Brady, all the way through the sixth round. Oops.

David Shapell and **Ralph Nobles** died. They were both 94 years old. There are some other ironic similarities. David Shapell was a Jewish immigrant and Holocaust survivor from Poland who worked hard and became a wealthy real estate developer and then gave millions of dollars toward the remembrance of the Holocaust. Ralph Nobles was a nuclear physicist who worked on the Manhattan Project, which of course was the atomic bomb, which led to the surrender of the Japanese empire in World War II. Both these men knew about mass deaths and war and the ugliness of human nature unleashed.

It's important to remember that about human nature unleashed, as we are seeing even now in our own century, and so it has been in every single year of human existence, it's just that now the technology is greater and the restraints fewer. So we have to teach how bad man can be, in a way that even an eighth grader can understand. But if you teach these eighth graders that "people are basically good" you're damaging them, you're lying to them, you're paving the way for their destruction, for the best case scenario is that people are a mix of good and bad, but the experience of history and the testimony of all the great world religions and philosophies is that we're born with a proclivity for bad and we better do everything we can to rein that in, or it's curtains for any civilization.

~

Leonard Nimoy died. He was 83. Everybody in the world knows him as Mr. Spock from *Star Trek*. When he started out on that show, it probably seemed like a good way for an actor to make some money, running around in a colorful tunic and pointy ears and saying wise things. He would then go back to serious acting, on stage or screen. It didn't quite work out that way, and Nimoy became so identified with the role that it altered his choices forever.

He tried to break away by writing a book called *I Am Not Spock*. That didn't work out the way he wanted it to. It seems he was, and always would be, Spock. So he eventually made peace with it and wrote a book called *I Am Spock*. Dueling autobiographies.

He also wrote a lot of poetry and did voice-over work. But most of his money came from the *Star Trek* movies and appearances. And that's really not a bad life after all, to have people look at you and think of you as an iconic character. Well, maybe for some. For others it didn't turn out quite so well. There was George Reeves, who was in *Gone with the Wind* and *From Here to Eternity*, but took on the role of Clark Kent and Superman in early television. There was no way he was going to break out of that. Everywhere he went kids would see him and shout, "Hey Superman!" TV in those days was merciless in branding an actor. It used to be said that if you became a star on TV you could never break into the movies. There were some exceptions. Steve McQueen did it.

James Garner did it. So did Clint Eastwood. George Reeves never got back into the movies, and died under suspicious circumstances. Did he shoot himself? Most people think so. And that was really troubling to so many children in America. Superman was dead, by his own hand. The bullet didn't bounce off him.

~

Anthony Mason died, and he was only 48, and I say that because he had been a star athlete, a professional basketball player with the New York Knicks during a time when they had a team contending for championships. Anthony Mason was not what they call a "finesse player." He was this big, strong, bowling-ball muscles package of ferocity who played defense like it was the Battle of Thermopylae. His aim was to take another player down, and he often did that with elbows to the stomach, chest or face.

I hate players who use their elbows as weapons. They are cheap-shot artists, hooligans in athlete's clothing, cheaters, mugs, cowards. I say that because I was on the receiving end of some elbows when I played the game, which I tried to play clean, and you're at a disadvantage when you play clean against a cheating punk. The first time it happened to me was in high school and I was guarding a power forward who played for a crosstown rival, and I was on him like stink on old cheese.

His answer to my masterful defense was to go up for a shot leading with an elbow to my chin. My bell rang, as they say, and there was a time out called and I went over to the bench and blood was pouring out of my mouth. The jerk had pushed my bottom teeth into my tongue and a big chunk of it was cut. In those days you didn't come out just because of a little blood, so I kept putting a white towel in my mouth to stop the bleeding, and my coach, not the Rod McKuen type, not the soft cushion, armchair child nurturer sort, didn't say much of anything to me, but told me to go back in.

So I finished that game, showered, went home. I got a piece of celery from the refrigerator and salted it up and bit into it. *Twang!* An electrical jolt zapped me from my front tooth to the back of my head. Turns out that blow to my chin sent my bottom teeth upward, chipped the back half of one of my front teeth, so I had to go to the dentist the next day and get the thing sawed down and a cap put on it. For years after that I had two front teeth that were not exactly the same color.

I still get mad when I think of that crud bucket. He was a dirty cheater and I hope he got spanked by an even bigger cheater, learned his lesson, and became a monk.

The other elbow incident happened the day before I got married.

Somehow the most beautiful woman in Los Angeles had consented to bind herself to me in holy matrimony. All the plans were in place. She had her gorgeous dress and Maid of Honor. I had my suit and Best Man. The church was booked, the invitations answered.

. . .

What did I do the evening before? I went to a sort-of bachelor party, a bunch of guys playing hoops down at Taft High. On the court that night was a big bruiser, a white guy about six-nine with oversized arms. I'm quite sure he did not speak English. I believe his native language was Grunt. He could have been a Neanderthal that had been frozen during the Paleolithic era, resuscitated in 1979 and was just now learning to play basketball, which he mistook as a competition for food.

In any event, this Neanderthal playing in a *pick-up game* decided this was his last chance for survival among the bipeds, and proceeded to throw an elbow in my face. He got me in the eye and cheekbone, and I told this Frankenstein monstrosity what he could do with himself and we had to be pulled apart, and then I walked out of that gym, because it was certainly not basketball being played by the last of his herd.

Of course, the next day, the wedding day, the biggest day of my life, I had one choice shiner, which we tried to cover with makeup, which made it through the ceremony, but in the photos of the reception, as the day wore on, you can see that the makeup had faded and it looked like my new bride had decided to hit me with a champagne bottle after an argument around the wedding cake.

So there's another memory that heats my cheeks, of that hulking slab who threw his cheating elbow at me the night before my marriage, but I believe he eventually migrated back to the Serengeti, where he foraged for grubs and gnawed on the rotting carcasses of dead gnus, until one day a lion challenged him for a hyena bone and he threw an elbow at the lion's face, and the lion tore him to bits. Or something along those lines.

Dwight Grell died at the age of 77. He was, says the *Times* of Los Angeles (a once-great newspaper), a collector of Russian ballet memorabilia. He had one of the largest collections in the world, but this was not the result of spare millions being spent, because Grell was a manager at a button factory most of his working life. At the end he was a ticket taker at an AMC movie theater. What he did was for love, and that's the best reason to do just about anything.

He loved the ballet, oh yes, was admittedly obsessed by it, but did not find that strange, for there are fans obsessed with their football teams and no one finds that odd, except in the strange case of Harvey Updyke, a raging fan of the Alabama Crimson Tide football program, a man who had Alabama colors all over his home, and who held a deep, burning hatred for Alabama's great rival, Auburn. This is where love can go too far, where the jealous lover becomes a stalker, where young Werther gets into his yellow vest and shoots himself over a woman. (*The Sorrows of Young Werther* was, by the way, the first break out fiction bestseller, a short novel by a young Goethe that so captured the German imagination that young men began shooting themselves for lost love, a development which disgusted Goethe, but was perhaps the first demonstration of the power of popular art to affect behavior), and so he decided he'd had enough of the crowing of victorious Auburn fans at their sacred oaks located at Toomer's Corner. This was the gathering place of Auburn students and boosters, the two beautiful oak trees providing inspiration and leaves. One night

Updyke drove spikes into the trunks, spikes which held a deadly poison, and he killed those trees. He was nabbed and eventually did some time in the can. Auburn had the trees replaced.

But dude, when you let your love become the thing that controls you, you're on the brink of insanity, which is really how love was classically portrayed. I mean, you have this cherub with a naked butt and bow and arrow, named Cupid, and when he hits you the love takes you over, just like that poison took over those oak trees, you're a goner, you're a nut, and if you don't watch out you'll act like a nut and maybe do something stupid.

By all accounts, Mr. Grell did nothing stupid, he just kept on collecting, and now that collection is safe and secure within the walls of the University of Southern California, where I went to law school, and for whose football team I root.

As for collections, I am not obsessive, though when I was a kid I loved comic books and *Mad* magazine, and especially *Classics Illustrated* which were comic book renditions of classic works of literature, which is how I became acquainted with *The Hunchback of Notre Dame, The Count of Monte Cristo, The Three Musketeers, Robin Hood, Men of Iron, Two Years Before the Mast, Mutiny on the Bounty*, and many more.

When I got to junior high the teachers all thought I was so well read!

· · ·

Mutiny on the Bounty reminds me of the *Mad* satire of the 1962 film starring Marlon Brando. My favorite feature in *Mad* was their satires of movies and TV shows, where the great artist Mort Drucker rendered the best caricatures known to man, and the satires always had great titles. This one was *Mutiny on the Bouncy*. Others I recall are: *Voyage to See What's on the Bottom; Flawrence of Arabia; Hack, Hack Sweet Has-Been; The Agony and the Agony; Who in Heck is Virginia Woolfe?; Botch Casually and the Somedunce Kid.*

∾

Don Johnson passed on. Not the actor. The ballplayer. He was 88. When he was twenty, he was a can't-miss pitching prospect for the New York Yankees. They said he had a fastball like Feller, and if you know anything about baseball you know that Feller's fabulous fastball flamed.

So he joined the Yankees and won a World Series ring in 1947. But then he got hurt, and his arm was never the same. He also liked the ladies and the liquor. Things just got worse. As the *New York Times* said: "Along the way, he pawned his World Series ring when his car broke down in Wyoming; was thrown in jail in Tijuana, Mexico, after a brawl; and was consigned to six days on a Florida chain gang after a drunken auto accident."

And so life goes, but when he was around 83 or so he came to an Old Timers Day at Yankee Stadium and got to wear the uniform and hear the cheers again, which never loses its flavor. He was interviewed by a reporter, and told him there were no regrets, he got to play with the best players of all time, like DiMaggio, Yogi Berra and Phil Rizzuto.

"Joe DiMaggio liked me," Johnson said. "He took me under his wing and said, 'Stay off the booze and away from the broads.'"

The reporter asked Johnson if he took DiMaggio's advice.

"Hell, no," said Don Johnson.

And speaking of Joe DiMaggio, those who saw him play said he was the smoothest center fielder there was, he would almost float to where the ball was going and gather it in, and then he'd come to the plate with the most beautiful right-handed swing ever, and rip those hits, one time doing that in 56 straight games, a record they say will never be broken. The closest anyone ever got to that was Pete Rose, who hit in 44 straight, and Willie Keeler, who did 45, and maybe you've never heard of Keeler, nicknamed "Wee Willie," because he played so long ago and was fond of telling people what the key to his hitting success was: "Hit 'em where they ain't."

Wee Willie Keeler is in the Hall of Fame, as is Joe DiMaggio, but Pete Rose is not because he got caught betting on baseball games, including those played by his own team, and that is against the rules, and then he lied about it and got caught lying, and that's all a shame, because the Hall of Fame has drunks and womanizers and racists in it, but not Pete Rose, who was one of my favorite players when I was a kid. Pete Rose should be in the Hall of Fame, because it's not about being a louse or a liar, it's about being a ball player, and that's what he was, one of the top ten players who ever lived.

Who is the greatest baseball player of all time? When I was a kid my dad and grandfather had no hesitation. I recall asking my dad, in the presence of my grandfather, who it was, and Dad said, "Tyrus Raymond Cobb!" And that was from my father who saw Babe Ruth hit a home run in Yankee Stadium when he was a boy.

Ty Cobb was a terror who sharpened his spikes and slid into bases spikes high to scare the basemen. Babe Ruth was a drinker and carouser who ate a lot of hot dogs and got fat. Ty Cobb was the best hitter, but Babe could hit for power, for average, and before that he was one of the best *pitchers* ever. He was an amazing baseball specimen. So I'm going to give the best-ever nod to the Bambino, the Sultan of Swat, the Colossus of Clout, Mr. George Herman Ruth.

Monroe Freedman died. He was 86. He was a law professor credited with making legal ethics an actual course of study for law schools, rather than something that is picked up on the street, or in the courtroom. I remember reading his stuff when I was in law school, and all the potential problems that could arise between a lawyer, his client, and the judicial system. For example, a poor guy is charged with a crime, the court appoints a lawyer for him, and the lawyer could think, Eh, I'll just plead the guy to a lesser charge, take the county's money, and not spend too much time on the case.

Or, if there was a trial, the lawyer could just go through the motions.

Well, Monroe Freedman wanted lawyers like that to lose their licenses, so he pushed for minimal standards, like, if you take a case, you're expected to really represent your client zealously.

This is especially crucial for criminal defense lawyers because, ladies and gentlemen, the client is almost always guilty. This isn't a Perry Mason world. In the real world a prosecutor doesn't file a case—most of the time, that is—unless it's a pretty sure bet the guy did it.

Of course, there are times when a prosecutor files, or over charges, because there's political pressure from mobs in the street. These kinds of prosecutors are gutless and a disgrace to the whole enterprise of justice.

There's also something called "plea bargaining," which is another ethical conundrum. Because, real world again, if a guy wants to take his chances with a jury, a guy who is clearly guilty based upon the evidence, then a judge is likely to hammer him at sentencing time, partly out of spite because the guy did not take a plea deal. And the plea deal itself is just to spare everybody the time and trouble of an actual trial, even though it says right there in the Constitution that everybody is entitled to a trial if that's what they want.

Mr. Freedman also fought for the right of lawyers to advertise, which is how we got "Better Call Saul" lawyers, and Larry Parker, who advertised in L.A. for many years, snarling at the camera, "I'll FIGHT for you," and for a while he had his clients on camera sort of winking at the audience and saying, "Larry Parker got me twenty million dollars." Like that was always going to happen. And as a criminal defense lawyer I wondered if I'd ever have a commercial, where a former client would look at the camera and say, "Jim Bell got me twenty years in San Quentin."

But I digress. There are some real important issues that come up, like this one: what if you know your client is going to lie on the witness stand? He outright tells you that. Now what do you do?

Professor Freedman said the lawyer-client privilege comes first, so you don't say anything. You let the client lie.

That did not sit well with the judges. No less than the Chief Justice of these United States, Warren Burger, said Freedman should be disbarred.

But maybe Freedman's biggest rant was against someone who did not exist. Monroe Freedman wrote a series of articles attacking none other than Atticus Finch, the central character in Harper Lee's masterpiece, *To Kill a Mocking*bird. Freedman claimed Finch was just a lazy white lawyer who took on the defense of a black man, Tom Robinson, only because he was asked to do so by a judge. In other words, Finch was some sort of closet cracker.

He caught a lot of heat for that. But guess what? Harper Lee, author of *To Kill a Mockingbird*, may have let Monroe Freedman off the hook. Too bad he died before her "lost" novel, *Go Set a Watchman*, came out in mid-2015.

Strangely unedited (it renders a different version of the Tom Robinson trial, for example), the novel is primarily about one thing—a daughter's coming to terms with her less-than-perfect father.

That's the big shocker everyone talked about: In *Watchman*, Atticus Finch is revealed to be a segregationist. He does not want the government or the courts telling him or his community how to live. He thinks the Supreme Court is using the Fourteenth Amendment to erase the Tenth Amendment. And he believes the black population is not ready for the responsibilities of citizenship.

In *Watchman*, Atticus is a member of the Citizens' Council of Maycomb County, a group of white men strategizing on how to deal with *Brown v. Board of Education*, and the NAACP and northern progressives.

The grown-up Jean Louise Finch (Scout from *Mockingbird*) discovers this about the father she idolized as a child. It all leads to the climactic scene—a knockdown argument between Jean Louise and Atticus over the "negroes."

"Let's look at it this way," Atticus says. "You realize that our Negro population is backward, don't you? You will concede that? You realize the full implications of the word 'backward', don't you?"

Jean Louise is horrified and responds: "You are a coward as well as a snob and a tyrant, Atticus." She goes on to compare him to Hitler and admittedly tries to grind him into the ground.

As a historical document, originally written in the mid-50s, *Watchman* is reflective of so many similar confrontations that took place back then—college-educated white children coming home to challenge their parents' views on race, especially in the South.

I will not reveal what happens in the last chapter. Suffice to say I was simultaneously moved and unsatisfied by it. Which may be the very point Harper Lee, the author, intended to make.

We live in an imperfect world, loving imperfect people. *Watchman* does not destroy the Atticus Finch of *Mockingbird*. Rather, it renders him flawed and therefore human.

You know, like the rest of us.

. . .

Jesus taught people to hate sin, but love sinners. In a world of so much hate, this message is exactly what we need to hear. Harper Lee's novel, so long locked up in a safety deposit box, may therefore be more important than we think.

And those are my thoughts on the passing of law professor Monroe Freedman.

There was another law professor I knew, named Michael Josephson, who was here in L.A. at Loyola, and ran a Bar review course I represented and sold to students at USC, so I could take it free.

The Bar exam. A two-day ordeal to test the mettle of would-be lawyers, so intimidating that a goodly percentage, maybe 20% in those days (I'm trying to remember) did not pass. I knew one guy, a former California Highway Patrol officer, who took the test four times and failed each time. Some people just cannot take tests, they freeze up, and after the first and second fail, it's in their heads for good, just like the putting yips get in the heads of golfers.

So I took Josephson's Bar review course, studied my tail off, and also got into shape. I'd been a fan of the great American chess player, Bobby Fischer, who captivated the country well before he turned into an anti-Semitic nutcase. He was the first American to defeat a Russian grandmaster for the World Championship, and before that big match against Boris Spassky he went into physical training because it was good for his brain.

So I did the same thing, with my lovely wife riding a bike alongside me as I ran and did wind sprints.

I was to take the Bar in Pasadena, a good twenty-minute drive, if traffic was good, from where we were living, so a friend offered me an unfurnished apartment right there in Pasadena, because her dad owned the building, and I took a mat and sleeping bag and set myself up in this place, and the night before I did not cram or study at all, I wanted to rest my mind, so I went to the movies. I saw *The Muppets Take Manhattan*. I got a good night's sleep, had a high protein breakfast at a diner, then went to take the test. And the next day, too.

It was torture waiting for the results. They were mailed around Thanksgiving, and my wife had the envelope waiting for me when I got home, and we were sweating hand grenades as I opened the envelope. I took out the letter and put the envelope over it so I could read it line by line. I got to *Dear James S. Bell*. Then I slipped the envelope down to the next line, my hands shaking, my throat dry, and saw the word *Congratulations*, and whooped. My wife whooped. We grabbed each other and whooped. We danced around the living room, whooping.

I was a lawyer.

.   .   .

I liked being a lawyer, like my father before me. I liked the idea of fighting for justice. I liked getting into the stacks of books (this was before the internet, you understand, and digitized law books), searching out precedent and weaving together a legal argument. I felt like Paul Newman in *The Young Philadelphians*, a movie about a working-class guy becoming a lawyer, and then defending a friend of his, played by Robert Vaughn, on a charge of murder.

The courtroom is a natural arena of conflict that has provided the blood and sinew of legal thrillers of every type. So many things can happen in a real court of law, not all of them desirable, such as the lawyer who, in the heat of battle, challenged a witness with, "And is that the same nose you broke as a child?"

Another lawyer asked a witness, "How many times have you committed suicide?"

Or this exchange:

Q: Now, Mrs. Johnson, how was your first marriage terminated?

A: By death.

Q: And by whose death was it terminated?

Lawyers. You gotta love 'em.

Deedee Corradini died. She was 70 years old, and the first woman to be elected mayor of Salt Lake City, which is a fine record to hold, because it was based on merit and not because she was a woman, for she convinced voters she could do a better job than the guy she was running against and the voters said, We will let you try! She did pretty well, too, helping to get the 2002 Winter Olympics to her city, only later she was named in a scandal about bribing Olympic officials, though she was never charged, so should be given the benefit of the doubt, something you don't get on Twitter.

She died of lung cancer, even though she never smoked, and that is one of those things, like the runner who is in great shape dropping dead at age fifty because his ticker was handed down to him by generations of bad tickers, and there's just not a darn thing you can do about that.

There are many people who get lung cancer because they smoke cigarettes, we all know that, but there is new hope for smokers who want to quit, and it's called vaping. They can switch to water vapor with nicotine in it, and nicotine doesn't affect the lungs, but guess what, friends and neighbors, there are people out there (and by out there I mean mostly New York and California in governmental positions) who want to eradicate vaping because … well, because … well, there's no good reason. Vaping is harmless, you see, and there's no such thing as second-hand vapor. Yet these folks are all for legalizing marijuana, but let's keep that demon water vapor at bay! And if more people die of lung cancer because of this? No problem! Fire up a joint and forget all about it.

~

Natalia Revuelta Clews died. She was 89, a Cuban, and was a knockout beauty in her youth, back there in Havana, and married a wealthy and prominent surgeon, but got caught up with revolution talk, and there wasn't a better talker than a fiery gent named Fidel, Castro that is, and when Castro got jailed for a failed attack on a military base, Natalia wrote him love letters and he wrote back to her. Oh yes, he was married at the time, too. And one time one of his letters to Natalia accidentally went to his own wife. Oops.

When Castro got out of prison he headed for Natalia and they consummated their passion. Castro went on to Mexico and asked his mistress to come with him, but she said no. She was also pregnant with their child.

And so life becomes like a novel, doesn't it? How many times have we heard this story? And its ending. After Castro seized power he became more interested in that than his former mistress and the mother of one of his children, and that was that. The scraggly-bearded, cigar-smoking revolutionary dumped her, leaving her alone and embittered (her surgeon husband had divorced her by then).

. . .

But she made it to 89, while Fidel is still, as of this writing, kicking it somewhere in Cuba. I think it's a *Weekend at Bernie's* thing going on, but that's just me.

Which brings up the subject of mistresses, and a simple, undeniable fact of history: so much of what has gone wrong in the story of mankind is due to the mayhem unleashed by unimpeded male lust, the unfettered fecundity of the voracious masculine appetite. The entire reason for marriage under God was to keep the polygamous predilection of the average man channeled toward but one woman and the children she bore him. He needed a "Thou shalt not commit adultery" stapled to his brain, and the threat of consequences that go with its violation.

But all too often the thing—you know, the *thing*—has led the man around like a slave master with a whip. And then what happens? Paris runs off with Helen, or Mrs. Menelaus as she was known in Sparta. You get the whole dang Trojan War.

Daniel von Bargen died, probably by his own hand, at the age of 64. He was an actor, best known for the role of Mr. Kruger on *Seinfeld.* Kruger was George Costanza's boss when he worked at Kruger Industrial Smoothing. He had struggled with diabetes, had a leg amputated, and they were going to chop more off him, and he apparently couldn't face that prospect.

There are people who do not get what they deserve, whether that be good or ill, if you look at things from a justice point of view, from the perspective of a biped walking around in time by pure chance. But there is reason to believe we are not here for the short span of life and then become worm food, and that there is a real justice, a true justice, that comes when our biped days are over, and there better be, for as my man Fyodor, as in Dostoevsky, put it, if there is no God, then anything in this life is permissible. That makes for a good, practical reason to believe in the here-after, but does that make it true in fact? You can't spot it with a telescope, but does that render it untrue?

Why do we have a moral conscience at all? Evolution? Look, there is such a thing as a Darwinism of the Gaps, where every single thing that we have that is counterintuitive to a survival of the fittest scenario is chalked up to some phantom "adaptive advantage" two million years ago, but which can never be seen with a telescope, either, but is taken on faith which sounds, gee, like a religious sentiment.

I find Jesus, and Isaiah, Amos, Ezekiel, Daniel, and Obadiah to be a knockout group of witnesses about where our moral sense comes from. As a former trial lawyer, I'd be hard pressed to find this whole crowd mendacious, stupid, or insane.

Sam Simon died. He was 59. But when he was 33 he helped bring a legendary show to TV, *The Simpsons*. He went on to win nine, count 'em, nine Emmy Awards. Not a bad run. He left *The Simpsons* in 1993, just as the show was hitting its stride, which only lasted until 1999 or so, when it suddenly became unfunny. But in those early years, *The Simpsons* was classic comedy with many of the episodes vying for the best of the best. There was the show about Kamp Krusty, the show about Homer building a backyard pool, the one about Homer going into the snowplow business, or when he became a founding member of the B-Flats (who knew Barney could sing like that?).

Along the way the show also gave us spot-on cultural types, my favorite being the Comic Book Guy, arrogant because, in part, he had a Master's Degree in Folklore and Mythology.

And of course, the manager of the Kwik-E-Mart, Apu Nahas-apeemapetilon. And the longsuffering principal of the Simpson kids' school, Seymour Skinner, whose dark experiences in 'Nam left him living with his mother and stalking the kids (which reminds me of another great episode, one of the Halloween specials, where Skinner leads the teachers in separating out plump children for, um, dietary purposes).

In short, the show was brilliant ... until it wasn't anymore, and that's how people and shows overstay their welcome, that's how a tired and stiff Willie Mays sadly ends his career with the Mets, of all teams, and Jordan with the Wizards, and most heavyweight boxers who have enough brains left, just not enough to say *no* to boxing again.

The old theatre adage is, always leave them wanting more, but when you have a show that's cheap to produce and people keep watching it, what the heck?

·   ·   ·

I'm glad Sam Simon got out while the getting was good, but sad he died at such a young age. He had more to write, more laughs to create, and we always need more laughs.

Isaac Heller died. He was 88 and the co-founder of a toy company named Remco, which was big during my childhood. They made things like the Whirlybird helicopter, and marketed them to boys with the ad phrase, "Fly them from battlefield to battlefield!" There was even a phrase that repeated on TV and on boxes and billboards and signs: "Every boy wants a Remco toy!" Later on, they started making dolls, and added the phrase "...and every girl, too!"

Because, you see, there once was a time when boys and girls were considered somewhat different, and that boys were supposed to grow up into brave men, in case the civilization needed protection from bad people who wanted a lot of Americans to die.

My toys of choice as a lad were plastic models—especially the models of Universal movie monsters, like Dracula and The Mummy—and games, I liked games, like Stratego, though I wasn't a big fan of Monopoly, I was never that good at buying and selling and I'd always land on Park Place when it had a hotel, and all I owned was a utility or some dismal street that was green.

I was never into military stuff, like a lot of my friends. I had some army men, but they didn't do much when I was awake (see *Toy Story* for what they may have done when I was asleep). My father was a Navy man, but only my oldest brother followed in those footsteps, doing a couple of years on the sea, on an aircraft carrier, in the years just before the Vietnam war took off under President Lyndon Baines Johnson.

My middle brother was in college when things got hairy in 'Nam, and I was just going into high school and by the time I registered for the draft the war was coming to a close.

It's a tough thing, a bad thing, a horror in fact, war, but nothing that can ever be eradicated even with Coca-Cola trying to teach the world to sing in perfect harmony. It's just not in the nature of mankind, and that means a nation that is committed to good things—yes, there are certain things that are good, like freedom, and certain things that are bad, like mass murder—has to keep raising up tough men to be able to fight in wars, as terrible a prospect as that is, but what is the alternative when bad people want to kill us and are willing to blow themselves up to do it?

Life is not made up of toys, but people, and many of those people are evil. They won't go away if we wish it, they won't suddenly become good if we just send out "good thoughts," as Richard Gere once suggested on an Oscar telecast. Happy thoughts will not end wars. Children can play with toys and all is well. Grown-ups have to leave the nursery at some point.

Maybe Mr. Heller and Remco were actually doing some good.

∾

Sir Terry Pratchett died. He was only 66 and died of early-onset Alzheimer's, which is a real tragedy to a mind that thought up fantasy worlds that pleased millions of readers over the years. His friend, the author Neil Gaiman, wrote about the advance of the terrible disease a few months before Pratchett died: "As Terry walks into the darkness much too soon, I find myself raging too: at the injustice that deprives us of - what? Another twenty or thirty books? Another shelf full of ideas and glorious phrases and old friends and new, of stories in which people do what they really do best, which is use their heads to get themselves out of the trouble they got into by not thinking? ... I rage at the imminent loss of my friend. And I think, 'What would Terry do with this anger?' Then I pick up my pen and start to write."

That is a fine tribute to Pratchett, a real writer, a prolific writer, who even sported a Hemingway-esque white beard. It's a ripoff that something took his mind and then his life, just as it is a ripoff when a good father or mother or sister or brother is taken away before a ripe old age.

There are young men who seem old, and old men who seem young, and women the same, and you like to see the young ones grow into old ones who still have a gleam in their eyes, like my friend Ralph Thomas, one of the founding members of the church I attend, a Gideon he was for many years and he's 103 years old now, he saw most of the 20th Century, and up until he hit his own century mark he was still sharp and funny, though it took a little longer for his comeback lines to make it from his brain to his vocal chords, but during that journey you could see in his eyes that it was coming. He got hammered by Father Time and is in a nursing home, and cannot speak, but he can look at you, and his eyes still dance, and that's something, boy.

Pratchett created a place called Discworld and wrote humorously and prolifically about it, for his entire span as a professional writer. Some writers can do that, stay in one place, like Faulkner did with Yoknapatawpha County, or Chandler did with Los Angeles. Ross Macdonald, whose real name was Kenneth Millar, did it with Santa Barbara, only he renamed it Santa Theresa so he wasn't tied down to real details unless he wanted to be, and that same locale has been taken over by Sue Grafton, who has private eye Kinsey Millhone in Santa Theresa, which is where I happened to go to college, the University of California at Santa Barbara.

Talk about a fantasy world. There is a little town called Isla Vista, right next to the campus, and it was filled with boys and girls who were moving from adolescence toward adulthood, which is a rocky, storm-tossed strait where many have drowned, and that happened at UCSB, not in the ocean, but in drugs and alcohol and promiscuity—there were those who did not make it out of there alive, and others who did not make it out of there whole. One of them was a guy I knew from high school, smart kid, cool kid, he was going to go to Harvard Law School, that was his goal, and he had the goods to get there, but he got into the hemp, the ganja, the Mary Jane. He started showing up to classes with red-rimmed eyes and a silly smile on his face. I don't think he ever graduated. A few years after college I ran into him at our old high school. He was traveling around in a van with a dog. He still had a silly smile on his face.

. . .

The occasional silly smile is fine, but should probably last no more than five seconds.

~

Jimmy Greenspoon died. He was 67, and for 46 years was the keyboardist for the rock band Three Dog Night, which is a long time to be with a band, longer than most marriages. In those halcyon days for rock and roll Greenspoon also backed up Eric Clapton, Jimi Hendrix, and the Beach Boys, to name a few.

Three Dog Night had a bunch of hits early, like "Mama Told Me Not to Come," and maybe their most famous, "Joy to the World," which is not a rendering of the Christmas carol but a song about a bullfrog named Jeremiah who was a good friend and a connoisseur of fine wine. The song was actually written by Hoyt Axton and, according to legend, was made up on the spot in a producer's office when Axton had the music but not the lyrics. So Axton sang, "Jeremiah was a prophet..." and that just clunked to the floor, so he tried again, and put in "bullfrog" instead and it sounded good and right, so he kept it and built a song around it that makes no sense.

But lyrics did not have to make sense in those days, like they did in the 1940s when they told stories in song, or the 1950s when they lamented lost boyfriends and girlfriends. In the late '60s and beyond, the lyrics could be indecipherable, maybe because we were jettisoning a world that *had* made sense at one time, for this new experiment in not making sense, but at least having a good sound you could move to, or get baked to.

· · ·

The best of the nonsensical lyrics bands has to be Steely Dan, great hummable tunes with words that don't add up to anything but a mood, usually a dark mood, but you're not getting dark yourself because the tunes are upbeat, and that was their deal, a goof, but a fun goof with some of the greatest guitar solos ever— thank you Jeff Baxter and Elliott Randall. Randall did "Reelin' in the Years," which is the greatest air-guitar solo of all time. I've played it driving the car in L.A. traffic, I've played it on a pencil, but most famously I play it on a broom. Hand me any broom and put on the song and I kill the "Reelin' in the Years" guitar solo.

There's part of every person who wants to be a rock star for one night, go out on a stage and have a packed arena screaming for you, and you begin your licks slow, the lights low, and suddenly you break into the main line and the drums and bass and keyboard kick in, and the fans go crazy and you sing your big hit song.

But that's fantasy, even when it's real, because it's going to end, the applause always does, and you have to have something else going on in your own dark nights of the soul, because if you don't, no lights come on and it's cold.

Speaking of bullfrogs, and we were, the greatest cartoon ever made is *One Froggy Evening,* the Warner Bros. classic about the construction demolition worker who finds a metal box in a building tear down. Inside the box is a frog, still alive, who immediately starts singing "Hello! My Baby" with a hat and a cane.

·   ·   ·

This inspired beginning was probably some brainstormed moment in the fertile imagination of the writer, Michael Maltese. Who knows? Writers get ideas everywhere, sometimes in dreams, sometimes in the shower, and there it is, presenting itself to you and asking you to do something with it.

From this spark what did Maltese do? He wrote, and Chuck Jones directed, not just a classic cartoon, but a morality tale for all time. Greed, friends, it's all about greed and the destruction it brings, and then at the end of the cartoon, it happens all over again, this time in the future.

A lot of people think the cartoon *What's Opera, Doc?* is the greatest of all, but I disagree. Bugs Bunny was getting old and Elmer Fudd was hitting the bottle pretty hard. Try as they might, their performances lacked the sharp edges of their early years together. (Around this same time, allegations of Foghorn Leghorn's egg embezzlements surfaced, making this a difficult period for Warner Bros. animation).

Serge Malas died. He was 94. His obituary in the *Springfield News-Leader* begins this way:

Serge Malas joined his wife Anna and son Eddie in the Lord's house on his 94th birthday, Thursday, March 12th, 2015. Serge passed peacefully at Mercy Hospital, Spfld, Mo. He was born in Kaunas, Lithuania, to Vladimier and Olia Malaschitchevas. The last name was shortened to Malas as part of the proceedings, receiving American Citizenship in 1957. His early education taught him the skills he used throughout his life working as a Machinist, later owning his own shop, Malas Machine Shop, Spfld. Mo. During WWII Serge came to work for the American Army in the 56th Quarter Master Depot, Geissen, West Germany as a skilled Mechanic. His services there made him instrumental to the success of the US Army during the war. He even built a new 110ft flagpole for the Depot, which is still there today.

I find that name, Malaschitchevas, to be magnificent. Too long for the American tongue of that time, but feeling like a huge pasture back in Lithuania, full of cows and goats and sheep. I love it that this man helped the war effort, and built a flagpole for the home-town depot, which is still there to this day.

Jack Haley died. He was 51, a former professional basketball player. Succumbed to a bad ticker. He played for several teams in the NBA, but most notably the Chicago Bulls where he was friends with the infamous screwball Dennis Rodman, a "piece of work" as they say, who could rebound like a madman and was an integral cog on one of the Michael Jordan teams that dominated the era, and so Jack Haley was kept on the team, so some people whispered, in order to "babysit" Rodman, but that never sat well with Haley, who insisted he was there to play ball.

I met Haley twice, once at O'Hare Airport in Chicago when we were passing each other on the way to a plane. I knew it was Jack Haley because he went to UCLA, my team as a kid, when John

Wooden was the coach, and because Haley was 6'10" and kind of hard to miss. The other time was when he ran a basketball camp that my son attended, and it seemed to me that was where Haley really fit, working with kids, not babies (and there are those who put Rodman in that classification, but I digress). My son thought him a very cool guy, and was proud of the fact that when he won the three-point shooting competition, Jack Haley was watching with approval.

My son won that competition because I had taught him to shoot, I am going to say that with no false humility added, because I was the greatest shooter in the history of Parkman Junior High School and close to the same at Taft High School and for one season as a freshman on JV at the University of California, Santa Barbara, and if to that skill had been added about five more inches of height or one second more of quickness, I think I might have made it to the NBA, which would have been before the Dennis Rodman era, which would have been fine with me.

But when I was in seventh grade I had my father put a basket up on our driveway which was big and level and allowed me to shoot from all angles, and I would practice hours on end out there, even in the rain, and I taught myself to shoot a proper shot by studying basketball books and doing what they said, like keeping my elbow underneath and giving the ball perfect backspin, and that was my advantage over the kids who just went out and taught themselves to shoot any which way, elbows flying, sidespin. It's like when I teach writing and tell people to study the craft and learn what works before you go off and do something else, which might not work, and every now and then I get someone who says it's not a matter of learning, man, it's just a matter of doing, and quit trying to put rules on me, man, and then they go and write and what they come up with is the equivalent of an elbow-flying, sidespin shot that clanks off the rim or, worse, does not hit the rim at all, the kind of humiliation that used to bring out of the great basketball announcer Chick Hearn the voiced-with-surprised jibe, "Doesn't draw iron!"

Going back to John Wooden, I mentioned attending his basketball camp, and learning lessons from him and getting an autographed "Pyramid of Success." That was famous back in the day, an old-fashioned work ethic model that I call old-fashioned not because it's quaint and unhelpful, but because it is powerful and effective but unknown today when we think there's nothing new to learn about work and sacrifice, and when those two words are largely gone from the vocabulary of a couple of generations who have been given trophies just for participating, and who've been spoon fed self-esteem flakes growing up, and now can't understand why no one will hire them even though they can bounce Mario all the way through the Mushroom Kingdom, yo.

A very different generation, yo, from the one known to **Norma Lee Calhoun**, who died at age 83. Her obituary states she was from both Sandy Springs, GA and Horseshoe Bend, AR, which reminds me of the joke about the magician who did the saw-the-woman-in-half trick until his assistant quit and went off to live in Tulsa and Dallas, but Mrs. Calhoun was together in both body and spirit, for she served as an elementary school teacher for 37 years, and I'll bet she was just the kind of teacher any child would love to have, because you don't teach for that long without loving what you do and having a good reputation doing it. She was a member of the First Baptist Church of Horseshoe Bend, and was "preceded in death by her 9 siblings and also her husband of 56 years," and that adds up to a good, full life, and I am going to go out on a limb here and say that a big part of the reason for that is embedded in that item about church, because she strikes me as just the kind of good, church-going woman who quietly lived her faith according to the simple yet powerful admonition of Jesus Christ himself, that in order of importance we are to love the Lord our God, and love our neighbor as we love ourselves.

A smart aleck schooled in the law decided to question Jesus about that, to trap him so to speak, by asking him for the definition of "neighbor," you know, like some politician or con artist (or maybe there's no difference there), and Jesus told a story, one of the most famous ever told, about the Good Samaritan, and you ought to read it yourself if you never have, you can find it in the Gospel of Luke, Chapter 10, verses 30-37. That's how you should live, and that's how you get to be the kind of person who helps kids for 37 years and contributes to the community, and is not a boil on the butt of humanity, which is a condition that is becoming rampant.

Ib Melchior died. He was 97, and wrote one of my favorite movies as a kid, *Robinson Crusoe on Mars*. Melchior had the idea of taking classics of literature and placing them somewhere in the future, in outer space. He tried to get other movies going, like *Gulliver's Space Travels* and *Treasure Asteroid*. But for some reason those never took off.

.   .   .

He did, however, experience the Hollywood grinder, the place where fakes and charlatans and sharks swim around in the same sea, inviting writers to jump in and become chum, which many writers do because they so desperately want to be part of the motion picture or television industry.

Ib Melchior was tossing around concepts for movies and TV shows back in the '60s, and he alleged that two of them—*Star Trek* and *Lost in Space*—were taken (stolen) and produced without him receiving dime one. He got on the *Lost in Space* movie in 1998 as a "special advisor," but they denied him compensation so he went to court ... and lost, another old Hollywood story, where the studios have the deep pockets.

Ideas and concepts cannot be copyrighted or protected, so it is with great risk that a writer with ideas goes around pitching them. Because a good idea can be purloined and another writer hired and that's it for the first writer, and too bad, Charlie.

In the early '90s I was actively pitching stories, especially to one producer who was going around town promising writers that if he liked a concept, and it landed with a company, he'd get the writer in on the deal. Like a stupid baby, a big, two-hundred-pound baby with a law degree, I believed this and pitched him my best stuff. There were several, but my absolute favorite was called "Time for Skippy!" It was about a teenager who gets sucked into a TV and finds himself living in a sitcom of the 1950s. I thought that would make a great "fish out of water" movie. I still do. But I never heard from that producer again.

·   ·   ·

If I could go back in time (hey, there's a concept!) and talk to my baby self, I'd say, Dude, you can't protect your ideas, so write the screenplay and register it with the Writers Guild, and then go out and sell it.

But I was too anxious, and I trusted someone in Hollywood, someone I did not know, and that was not a smart move. Years later, I was asked out to lunch by a guy about my age. He was a screenwriter, and by most measures a successful one. Two of his scripts had been turned into hit movies. He made a lot of money doing rewrite work, which basically means you get notes from people who know nothing about writing and you have to do what they say, because they are the ones with the money and the clout and the deals to make movies happen.

He wanted to talk to me about self-publishing, which I had embraced and which was both a financial and creative shot in the arm for me. When I asked him why he wanted to do this, he said that the screenwriting world he inhabited was "soul sucking."

Fascinating. Here was a guy who'd had the kind of career I had once dreamed of having. If a fairy godmother had come to me in 1990 and offered me that career, I would have said, "Hit me, babe." But now here I was, hearing that this career was not all it was cracked up to be because his soul was disappearing into some cosmic Hoover.

I realized then that the career I actually have is the one I actually want.

. . .

So I feel for Ib, who was the son of a famous Dutch opera singer, a tenor named Lauritz Melchior, but he didn't want to follow in his father's footsteps because he thought if he made it big, people would say it was because of his father, and if he flopped they'd say, See, he was never as good as his father, so he went into the movie game instead, and what did he get out of it? He didn't even get an aria. He hardly got two bills to rub together.

Lauritz Melchior, by the way, was famous for singing Wagner. Now Wagner was an anti-Semite who wrote great music, and that always brings up the question of whether an artist's personal life and opinions should be part of the assessment of his art. I will tell you this, if that view is taken you can pretty much get rid of 80% of the paintings, songs, music, movies, books, stories, and chalk drawings in the world. I would like to enjoy more movies than I do, but I find myself taken out of them if the star of the film has made public statements that have the intellectual weight of a mosquito, which is many of them, or have personal lives that are about as inspiring as road kill, which is also many of them.

One of the best writers of the Hollywood scene is Joe Eszterhas, especially his book *Hollywood Animal*, which I read shortly after another book of that ilk (a great word, ilk) *You'll Never Eat Lunch in This Town Again* by Julia Phillips, and also *Hollywood Days, Hollywood Nights* by Ben Stein.

When I was starting out in the screenwriting game, Eszterhas was sort of a legend in Hollywood, the highest paid screenwriter of all. He fetched $3 million for a script called *Basic Instinct.* That was big news to us young scribes, and the reason why everyone in L.A. with opposable thumbs was writing a screenplay.

But what shot Eszterhas into the mythical stratosphere was what he did to a man named Michael Ovitz. If you are unfamiliar with that name, let me just say that Michael Ovitz was the most powerful agent in Hollywood, one of the partners in the huge upstart Creative Artists Agency. They had a powerful roster of stars, from Redford and Streisand to Cruise and Costner, and directors like Sydney Pollock and Martin Scorsese. They also had Eszterhas, the highest paid screenwriter, and many others like him. CAA gripped the industry like a banana, and Ovitz was the 1,000 pound gorilla.

You did not mess with Ovitz. He had a worn copy of Sun Tzu's *The Art of War* in his office, and so did all his employees. He looked upon Hollywood as a war zone, and he was the chief warrior. Everybody else in town thought so, too.

Joe Eszterhas had a friend named Guy McElwaine, an agent who'd helped him get started, left agenting, and was now back. Joe told Guy he'd be his client again.

Joe went to break the news to Michael Ovitz. Let's just say that Ovitz did not take it well. There was a meeting in Ovitz's office. According to Joe Eszterhas—who was so shaken by the meeting that he made copious notes while it was still fresh in his mind—

Mr. Ovitz said, No, Joe, you are not going to leave me. And if you try, "my foot soldiers who go up and down Wilshire Boulevard each day will blow your brains out." Then Ovitz said he would sue Joe and further, "I don't care if I win or lose, but I'm going to tie you up with depositions and court dates so that you won't be able to spend any time at your typewriter."

None of this surprised me at the time. This is how powerful Hollywood types always act. What surprised me, and everybody in town, was what Joe Eszterhas did about it. After initially caving in to the threats, he determined that he could not live with himself, let alone write scripts, with Ovitz representing him. Despite being warned by all sorts of people not to do anything, to just shut up and play along, Joe sat down at his typewriter and wrote a long letter to Ovitz. He then made copies of the letter, and made sure one of those copies was unsealed and sure to be opened up by a curious party and then leaked to the press.

Boy, did it leak. And boy did a storm follow.

In the letter Eszterhas detailed the meeting with Ovitz and another CAA agent named Rand Holston. At the time Eszterhas was close to a producer named Irwin Winkler:

To say that I was in shock after my meetings with you and Rand would be putting it mildly. What you were threatening me with was a twisted new version of the old-fashioned blacklist. I felt like the character in Irwin's new script whose career was destroyed because he refused to inform on his friends. You were threatening to destroy my career because I was refusing to turn my back on a friend.

I live in Marin County; I spend my time with my family and with my work; I've avoided industry power entanglements for thirteen years. Now I felt, as I told my wife when I came home to think all this over, like an infant who wakes up in his crib with a thousand-pound gorilla screeching in his face.

In the two weeks that have gone by, I have thought about little else than the things you and Rand said to me. Plain and simple, cutting out all the smiles and friendliness, it's blackmail. It's extortion, the street-hood protection racket we've seen too many times in bad gangster movies. If you don't pay us the money, we'll burn your store down.

After laying out his version of the facts, Joe Eszterhas made his decision clear:

What I have decided, simply, after this period of time, is that I cannot live with myself and continue to be represented by you. I find the threats you and Rand made to be morally repugnant. I simply can't function on a day-to-day business basis with you and Rand without feeling myself dirtied. Maybe you can beat the hell out of some people and they will smile at you afterward and make nice, but I can't do that. I have always believed, both personally and in my scripts, in the triumph of the human spirit. I have abhorred bullying of all kinds — by government, by police, by political extremism of the Left and the Right, by the rich —

maybe it's because I came to this country as a child and was the victim of a lot of bullying when I was an adolescent. But I always fought back; I was bloodied a lot, but I fought back.

It wasn't long before this letter was all over town, and Michael Ovitz was throwing a fit. Secretly, always secretly, people began to whisper to Joe Eszterhas their eternal thanks for calling out the 1,000 pound gorilla. But virtually everyone thought, in public, that Joe's career was over, that studios would be too frightened of Ovitz to work with him, that all the CAA stars would never appear in any of his scripts, and so on.

People started warning Eszterhas to watch his back, and his family, very carefully. In the Mafia sort of way. One person told him to leave the country. And, indeed, he did get death threats, whispered voices over the phone like in some Warner Bros. crime movie of the 1940s. One morning he found a skull-and-cross-bones bandana wrapped around his newspaper.

Later, when Joe and Guy McElwaine determined the source of these threats, they threatened to get the FBI involved, and the threats stopped.

A short time later Eszterhas sold *Basic Instinct* for a record sum. If you had written this as a movie script, no one would have believed it. But Ib Melchior could have placed it in the future on a some distant planet, and it would have been just fine.

～

Gregory Walcott died. He was 87. He was a tall, rugged actor who appeared in films with Clint Eastwood and other stars, and for directors like the legendary John Ford. But he will be forever remembered for one leading role, because it happened to be in what many consider to be the worst film ever made.

Plan 9 From Outer Space is a cult favorite, a space movie made by the notoriously talentless director Ed Wood. Tim Burton made a whole movie about Mr. Wood, a poetic and largely fictional account of his friendship with the dying Bela Lugosi, and the making of this movie with such bad special effects you can see tombstones wobbling and strings on the flying saucers. The Tim Burton movie, starring Johnny Depp as Ed Wood, turns out to be a touching meditation on the love of film, even if you don't have the goods to make a great one. My favorite scene in the Burton movie is when Ed Wood, who was a transvestite, is dressed up in his angora sweater and high heels and goes to Musso & Frank for a drink. He's frustrated because his investors want to control the shooting of *Plan 9*. And he sees, sitting alone at a table, the great Orson Welles.

He walks over to express his admiration. And Welles talks to him, director to director, without condescension. Welles shares Wood's frustration, as he is shooting a film called *Touch of Evil* and the studio wants Charlton Heston to play a Mexican.

Then Welles tells Wood to stick to his guns, his vision. And Ed Wood walks out inspired. It's a sweet, touching moment. The world's greatest director talking to the world's worst director.

·   ·   ·

The actual *Plan 9* is not so sweet or touching, except in knowing the backstory of its making. My favorite moment in *Plan 9* is when two detectives are in the graveyard trying to figure out the mystery. One of the cops has his gun out. And he proceeds to scratch his head with the barrel of the gun.

So there is Gregory Walcott, who took this role as a favor to a friend, thinking nothing of it, but oh, now he is associated with that film, and that bugged him no end for the rest of his days. "It's enough to drive a Puritan to drink!" he once said.

He served time in the Army before hitchhiking to Hollywood to try to make it as an actor. He was 6'4", so when hitching he held a tennis racquet in his hand, to give the impression he was a prep school tennis player, and that it was safe to pick him up.

He was married for 55 years, and had three kids and six grand-kids, and that's something that life gave him that overrides even his appearance in *Plan 9 From Outer Space*.

You take what is good and cherish it, and you ride out what is bad, and that is the description of life on this earth, and it's true whether you venerate and worship God or venerate and worship yourself, though one reason I go to church is that I find myself such a lame object of worship.

Elvin R. Clausen died. He was 89, a citizen of Sioux Falls, South Dakota. He had one of those old-fashioned country names, Elvin, and indeed he was born on a farm and educated in country schools. He got out of high school in 1943 and joined the Navy and served his country during World War II. He got home, got married, had eight children, worked for a distributing company, and lived his life according to those values that were taught to him in those country schools. His obit says he liked dancing and playing pinochle.

I've always liked the name of that game, pinochle, though I can't say I've ever played it. My card games are blackjack, poker, and hearts. When I was in college my roommates and I had killer hearts games, and then on Friday night it would be poker all night and into the morning at some venue or other, and that, of course, is how you get through college, right?

Then, once a quarter, after finals, we'd pile into a car and head to Vegas, usually getting one cheap motel room for four or five guys, and then playing high stakes, like 50¢ blackjack. I got to be pretty good at it, not counting cards but at least knowing what to play so the odds were almost even with the house. Then one day a neighbor of ours back in Isla Vista, the town next to the UCSB campus, came over to declare he had found a way to beat the house, by counting cards and keeping track of the count on a special, digital watch he'd made. He was looking for investors, and I was looking for an easy way to make money, so I gave him some dough—and I'm glad my dad never found this out—and off he went to Vegas. When he got back he reported he was busted, flat broke, that the watch didn't work.

· · ·

This was how I learned not to become a professional gambler or venture capitalist. I never thought I'd see that money again, but this neighbor was honorable and he actually paid me back over time. A rare thing these days, honor, which means doing something you know you ought to do even when you don't have to do it.

Some of my favorite movies are about honor, like *High Noon* starring Gary Cooper. In that movie Cooper plays a town marshal who has just retired and married Grace Kelly. Grace Kelly! Not Mildred Koppelheimer, but Grace Kelly, one of the most beautiful women ever to appear on the silver screen, so now he's going to go off with his bride and they'll open a store and live a quiet life.

But then comes the news. A killer this marshal had caught and testified against, and seen sent off to prison, was out by way of a pardon from the governor. Not only that, he had three of his gunman thugs waiting at the train station for him. He had pledged to come back and kill this marshal, Will Kane. Everybody in town tells Kane to leave, get on his buckboard and get out of town, no one will blame him.

So he does. But half a mile outside of town he stops. He tells his wife he has to go back. She doesn't understand that. She's a Quaker, and therefore against guns and violence. She pleads with him not to, but all he says is "I've got to. That's the whole thing."

. . .

That's what it means to have honor. You just do what's right, no matter the cost, because that's the whole thing.

~

Dr. George Fischbeck died. He was 92. For twenty years or so he was the weatherman for the local ABC station in Los Angeles. Wore a bow tie, seemed like the kind of science teacher you would have wanted in high school, and, in fact, that's what he was before he got into meteorology for profit. He had a quirky personality, which is what local weathercasters are supposed to have, until the brass started hiring women with, shall we say, curves, so they could stand in profile next to the weather map so that the men in the audience had a choice whether to look at the map or the meteorologist, with the latter easily winning over the temperature in Palm Springs.

Dr. George, as he was known, rendered his duties and was loyal to Los Angeles. I grew up in a time when they had local children's shows, like Bozo and Sheriff John and Engineer Bill and Skipper Frank and Tom Hatten (who showed Popeye cartoons). Once when my folks were driving and I was in the back seat of our car, which had one of those big bench back seats they had back then, my dad told me that Engineer Bill was behind us. I got on my knees and looked out the big back window and there he was, Engineer Bill himself! He drove a car that was made up to look like a train engine. I would have known him anywhere, a big moon face and glasses and a smile like a slice of the sun. And there I was, six or seven years old, and I waved at him. And he waved back! Engineer Bill waved back at me right there on Ventura Boulevard in Woodland Hills, California! I turned to my mom and dad and said, "He waved at me!" I turned once more to the window and waved again, and he waved back again! He smiled. Like he was enjoying this! I waved once more, and Engineer Bill waved back, and would have done so all the way to the end of the line, as the train guys say, because that's what it meant to be a kids' show host in those days. It was not like Krusty the Clown on *The Simpsons,* is another way of putting it.

And speaking of Engineer Bill, **Sheriff John** died at the age of 93. His given name was John Rovick, and he was another kids' show icon. Los Angeles local KTTV Channel 11 ran "Sheriff John's Lunch Brigade," which stayed on the air until 1970.

"Come on now, laugh and be happy and the world will laugh with you," he'd sing in a smooth baritone, lip-synching as he entered the door of the sheriff's office set at the beginning of each show. The opening included leading his young viewers in reciting the Pledge of Allegiance.

"We talked a lot about safety, courtesy, manners and things like that," he told the *Idaho Statesman* in 2005. "We often had firemen or police officers as guests, and I'd warn the kids not to do things like play in the street or get into refrigerators or play with matches."

He'd also do occasional live remotes, taking viewers to see how bread was made, or how cars were assembled at a GM plant in Van Nuys. And, of course, he'd show cartoons (those with Crusader Rabbit were early favorites).

·   ·   ·

One highlight of the show, whose primary target was 4- and 5-year-olds, was Sheriff John's reading of the names of dozens of viewers who were celebrating birthdays. Then he'd sing "The Birthday Cake Polka" — "Put another candle on my birthday cake. We're gonna bake a birthday cake ... Put another candle on my birthday cake, I'm another year old today!" — as a large cake revolved on a lazy Susan.

Sheriff John also had lunch along with his viewers—he'd usually eat a sandwich and have a glass of milk after saying a brief nondenominational prayer.

"It was a real good little prayer," he recalled in 2008 in the *L.A. Times*, the words still fresh in his mind: "Heavenly father, great and good. We thank thee for our daily food. Bless us even as we pray. Guide and keep us through this day."

Rovick once received a letter from a mother saying her young son had asked her how old Sheriff John was. She told him, "I don't really know." To which the boy said: "He must be hundreds of years old. Every day he sings, 'I'm another year old today.'"

One father wrote a letter of thanks and told him how his young daughter learned to say the Pledge of Allegiance: "... with liberty and justice for all, and now for our first cartoon."

There used to be a consensus about what was good for young children to watch. With eight million satellite channels now, that's pretty much out the window. Good parents must be ever vigilant. Bad parents do things like take their young children to horrific movies because they can't find a babysitter.

Back in 2002 I wrote a letter to the *Los Angeles Times,* occasioned by just this type of thing:

The country was rightly repulsed at the videotape of Madelyne Toogood beating her 4-year-old child in an Indiana parking lot. We know such mistreatment can have a terrible effect on a child's mental health. But how many Americans indulge in a worse form of abuse without a second thought? I'm talking about taking kids to the movies. The wrong movies.

The other night I saw *Red Dragon,* the third installment in the Hannibal Lecter series starring Anthony Hopkins. When the bad guy (Ralph Fiennes) bites off the tongue of a screaming reporter, then stands up, mouth bloody, and spits out the offending organ, I squirmed in my seat. What I couldn't stop thinking about, however, was the little girl in the seat in front of me.

She looked about 6 years old. I'd seen her waltz into the theater with her parents, tub of popcorn in hand, chirpy voice yakking it up excitedly. Two hours of mayhem ensued. People stabbed, set on fire, tortured. Your average day at the office for serial killers. Every now and then I'd lean over and see the little girl with her eyes fixed to the screen.

.   .   .

How times have changed. I remember going to the drive-in with my parents in the early 1960s. Then, about the worst thing you'd see onscreen was Godzilla stomping through screaming crowds in Tokyo, or Frankie Avalon pretending to surf. On occasion my mom put her hand over my eyes to keep me from seeing something she deemed too scary.

Now we have kids watching slashers, rapists and cannibals because Mommy can't be bothered with finding a baby-sitter, or Daddy is so clueless he doesn't see the difference between Disney and disemboweling.

After the movie, I waited outside the theater. I wanted to take a look at the happy trio as they emerged from this uplifting bloodbath. I wanted to glare at them, in fact. The little girl was being carried by the father. She was frozen. Her face was pale, her eyes wide. She looked like she was in shock.

Children are not just bodies that hurt when they're hit by the likes of Madelyne Toogood. They are souls, spirits in formation, for whom exposure to vile images does enormous damage. We used to believe in a long term of innocence for our kids, in protecting them from input only adults are wired to handle.

A 15-year study by Joanne Cantor, a professor at the University of Wisconsin, a recognized expert on children and the mass media and author of the book "Mommy, I'm Scared," concluded that disturbing images on television can lead to severe fright reactions that last for years, or a "deadening of emotional responsive-ness ... toward violence."

We think children should be protected from secondhand smoke but don't give a rip (you'll pardon the expression) if they're exposed to ritual murder and grotesque violence.

The solution is not that difficult. Have a small child? Think "G-rated." Or stay home. Rent *VeggieTales* or *Beauty and the Beast*. But leave Hannibal the Cannibal and his ilk to the adults who can handle him.

What became of this little girl? Did she overcome this nightmare? Or was this just the tip of that parenting iceberg, and did this child become a drug addict? Or was it something in between? There is a certain resiliency in children, but when it is relent-lessly hammered by bad parenting, or no parenting, it's a goner, it's like a wounded chicken alone in the henhouse when the coyote comes looking for lunch and some entertainment.

This letter ended up getting me as a call-in guest on a talk show hosted by Danny Bonaduce, who first came to fame as a child actor on a television show called *The Partridge Family*. So on this TV talk show the producers had me call in to discuss this matter during a chat about child rearing, and I told my story and then I said I considered this child abuse. To which Danny Bonaduce said, "Did you call the police?" And I said, "I didn't call the police because this conduct *isn't against any law*. But parents should be somehow held accountable for these kinds of actions."

. . .

Re-runs of *The Partridge Family* are actually a good alternative for kids' viewing.

~

Gene Saks died at the age of 93. He was a Broadway comedy actor and director, a three-time Tony Award winner, best known for working with Neil Simon on several of his plays. But I will always remember him for one, sparkling, hilarious acting job as Chuckles the Chipmunk, the insecure, high-strung host of a children's TV show in *A Thousand Clowns*. The movie, based on the play by Herb Gardner, is about one Murray Burns, a 1960s New Yorker who writes for the Chuckles the Chipmunk show. He is their best writer in fact, a joke factory, able to connect with the kids because Murray is a bit of a kid himself, an eccentric who collects eagle statuary. Murray is also raising his nephew, Nick, who was abandoned by his mother. As the movie opens, Murray has quit Chuckles because of job burnout and is living day-by-day, doing as he pleases, with Nick in tow. But now social services is closing in, to assess whether this lifestyle is in the best interest of young Nick, a kid with an outsized intelligence that often befuddles the stuffy social worker team that comes to Murray's apartment for an unannounced visit.

It's a brilliant movie, with Jason Robards playing Murray, and now he has to go find a job to keep Nick, but he is adamant about not going back to Chuckles, it was a mind-numbing, soul-sucking (there's that word again) job writing jokes for a manic children's show host who admits he "doesn't get along too well with kids." But Murray, as a man of that time, needs something more out of his work. He knows it's a matter of psychological life and death. He tries to explain this to his bland, working-man brother, Arnold:

Arnold, five months ago I forgot what day it was. I'm on the subway on my way to work and I didn't know what day it was . . . I was sitting in the express looking out the window, watching the local stops go by in the dark, with an empty head and my arms folded, not feeling great and not feeling rotten, just . . . not feeling. And for a minute I couldn't remember, I didn't know, unless I really concentrated, whether it was a Tuesday or a Thursday or . . . for a minute it could have been any day, Arnie. It scared the hell out of me. You've got to know what day it is. You have to own your days and name them, each one of them, every one of them, or else the years go right by and none of them belong to you.

Amen.

∽

Andrew Getty died. He was 47 and the heir to the billions built up by his grandfather, J. Paul Getty. At the moment they are calling it death by natural causes, but he also had blunt force trauma to the head, which means he either fell down and conked his head or was murdered, and as a thriller author, I can't help defaulting to that in my mind, for we are talking about a troubled man and billions of dollars, and when you put those two things together, especially in L.A., you get plot lines.

· · ·

The cops said that two weeks before his death Andrew Getty had sought a restraining order against "a woman," but his attorney declined to give further information. Does that not raise the thriller hackles on your neck?

J. Paul Getty, of course, made his money in oil and stocks. I don't think he had a happy life. One of his sons died by his own hand, and a nephew of his named J. Paul Getty III was kidnapped in Italy and held for ransom for more than five months. His ear was severed by the kidnappers and sent to the family. The family paid out $2.8 million and got him back. Several nappers were nabbed, but only two were convicted. The money was never recovered.

The Bible says, "Better is a handful with quietness, than both the hands full with travail and vexation of spirit."

One of the wealthiest men I knew did not live a happy life, even though he owned a prime piece property in one of the most exclusive sections of Los Angeles, and did not have to worry one bit about money—he could eat where he pleased, travel where he wished, dress however he liked, drive whatever he desired, and float his boat however he wanted it floated—but he had a bee in his bonnet, or a fly in his ointment, or a burr in his saddle, some cliché like that: he was convinced the IRS had taken more of his money than they deserved, and carried out a daily campaign of harassment aimed at IRS officials, politicians, attorneys general, news reporters, and anyone else he thought was complicit in or apathetic about his plight. He wrote so many letters they had to clear a rain forest in Brazil. He received letters in return, with yadda yadda language, so much so that I figured there was an entire office or cubicle or at least copy machine that was used exclusively to churn out responses to this one man, who never gave up until he issued his last breath on earth, and in that last breath probably uttered, "You owe me..."

It is not good to leave this life muttering, "You owe me..."

A man who made millions who did not go out that way was **Gary Dahl**, who died at the age of 78. He seemed a happy fellow with an agile mind, for he earned his millions by selling rocks to people. Yes, back in 1975, for a few weeks, a fad took over the nation—Pet Rocks. Dahl created a box that looked like a little pet carrier, with air holes and all, but inside was a rock. It even came with a little printed instruction book on the care of your Pet Rock. He sold those babies for four bucks, and apparently a million and a half people bought them.

This amused some and outraged others. The angry cried out, How dare he! Selling something worthless to people! And making real money at it! To which the old adage applies, *caveat rocktor,* let the rock collector beware. If people wanted to buy a joke, what's wrong with that? We need more jokes.

Some of my favorite jokes are the "walks into a bar" kind. Like:

.   .   .

Julius Caesar walks into a bar. He orders a Martinus. The bartender says, "Don't you mean a Martini?" And Caesar says, "If I wanted a double I'd've asked for it."

Guy walks into a bar with a piece of asphalt under his arm. He says, "I'll have a drink, and one for the road."

A horse walks into a bar and sits down. The bartender says, "Hey, buddy, why the long face?"

A skeleton walks into a bar and says, "I'll have a beer. And a mop."

Short jokes are best, the fastest way from point A to point L, for Laugh. The master of that kind of joke was Mr. Henny Young-man, whose line, "Take my wife ... please," has come into our language as a kind of mantra, though to be fair there are husband jokes, too, such as the woman who says, "I have a model husband. He's just not a working model." And the observation, "The only reason she's had nine children with him is she's trying to lose him in a crowd."

But nowadays you have to watch your jokes, because someone might get "offended." We used to have a much more enjoyable culture when people were big enough not to be offended at every off-hand hilarity. One of the tests of maturity is whether you can disagree without being offended. And if that is indeed the test, we are a nation of children.

.   .   .

If someone cracks a joke and you don't like it, don't run around trying to shut down speech. Just tell funnier jokes yourself.

Gary Dahl, by the way, also had another feather in his fedora, and that is this: he won the Grand Prize in the annual Bulwer-Lytton Fiction Contest, which gives an award for the best "bad" opening line. (In case you are unfamiliar with him, Edward Bulwer-Lytton was a popular British novelist of the mid-1800s, who gave us the oft-repeated-in-jest opening line *It was a dark and stormy night.* The full context of that line comes from a novel of his called *Paul Clifford,* which is a terrible title by today's standards but didn't bother the Brits of Bulwer-Lytton's time. It has a terrible opening paragraph:

It was a dark and stormy night; the rain fell in torrents—except at occasional intervals, when it was checked by a violent gust of wind which swept up the streets (for it is in London that our scene lies), rattling along the housetops, and fiercely agitating the scanty flame of the lamps that struggled against the darkness.

That's the sort of opening a writing teacher, such as your humble narrator, would decry and throw a fit over, for it is omniscient viewpoint with author intrusion, and that's just not done today, because the best fiction loses the author in deference to the story.

.   .   .

So somebody decided to have a Bulwer-Lytton contest where people could submit fake bad openings. Gary Dahl's winning entry:

The heather-encrusted Headlands, veiled in fog as thick as smoke in a crowded pub, hunched precariously over the moors, their rocky elbows slipping off land's end, their bulbous, craggy noses thrust into the thick foam of the North Sea like bearded old men falling asleep in their pints.

Wonderfully dreadful, that. By the way, one of my favorite entries from a Bulwer-Lytton contest is the following. I apologize to the author whose name I have lost, but if you are reading this, accept my belated congratulations:

With a curvaceous figure that Venus would have envied, a tanned, unblemished oval face framed with lustrous thick brown hair, deep azure-blue eyes fringed with long black lashes, perfect teeth that vied for competition, and a small straight nose, Marilee had a beauty that defied description.

And jokes, jokes! Oh, the land of jokes has suffered loss, the desert is more parched, the birds bereft of song, for **Tom Koch** has died at the age of 87! Who was this man? Only the main writer for one of the great comedy teams of all time, Bob and Ray, and if you do not know the comedy of Bob and Ray you really have no life to speak of, it is a life deprived, a life with a hole in it, and that hole can only be filled by listening to some of the bits of

Bob and Ray, especially *The Slow Talkers of America* bit which you can find online. Listen and laugh, for you will laugh, and that will restore your life to the fullness you wish it to have, and that was partly due to the writing of Mr. Koch and the impeccable timing of Bob Elliott and Ray Goulding.

Mr. Koch also wrote for *Mad* magazine and many classic TV comedy shows, making him a triple threat, a veritable Willie Mays of comedy writing. I remember one of his *Mad* bits, the invention of a complicated sport known as 43-Man Squamish. In part, it goes like this:

Rooted in Klishball and Stiffleball, Squamish is supposed to be played on a pentagonal field, or Flutney. Players can carry, kick or throw a spheroid Pritz, three and three-quarters inches in diameter, made from untreated ibex hide stuffed with blue jay feathers. They have five Snivels, or downs, within which to score, generally by running across the goal line (for a 17-point Woomik) or smacking the Pritz across the line with a Frullip, a stick shaped like a shepherd's crook and usually wielded by the defense to block the other team from scoring.

Classic *Mad* humor—intelligent, biting, hilarious, and accompanied by their great art work (in this case from George Woodbridge, who worked for *Mad* for 44 years!)

∽

Dr. Robert Schuller died. He was 88, a famous TV preacher for many years, who started his ministry at an abandoned drive-in movie theater. It was an innovative idea fitted for car-crazy Southern California. Folks could drive to church and stay in their cars! Put on the speaker, listen to the singing and the sermon. He drew a lot of people with his message of "Possibility Thinking" which, truth be told, was a not so subtle lifting of the "Positive Thinking" message of Dr. Norman Vincent Peale.

Speaking of whom (Peale, I mean), he was a major influence at a crucial time in my life.

One dismal summer day in 1979 I was standing on the corner of Hollywood and Vine. I'd just come from an audition and was heading back to my apartment. I paused on the most famous crossroads in Hollywood as a bus drove by and spewed a stream of black exhaust my way.

I'll never forget that moment. A wave of despair washed over me. I felt suspended over a dark abyss, with no one to pull me back. What was the point of all this? Like in the old Peggy Lee song, I wondered *Is that all there is?*

Feeling more than a little desperate, I walked down to Pickwick Bookshop on Hollywood Boulevard. I knew I had to find something to help me. I went to the religion section, thinking maybe what I needed was a recovery of my faith. I'd become a Christian in high school, but then I'd gone on to a college where religion was not exactly the hot item on campus. It wasn't long before I was into many of the things I'd heard happen at "party schools." Sundays were not for church, but sitting at the beach drinking beer and igniting certain plant life. I don't think I cracked open a Bible the whole time I was in college.

Now, three years removed from graduation, I was hoping that I could find in a book some relief for the darkness I now felt crushing my spirit. As I scanned the religion section I saw the name Norman Vincent Peale featured prominently. I'd seen the movie *One Man's Way* a few years earlier, the biopic about Dr. Peale. Well, I reasoned, they made a movie about the guy, he must have something going on.

So I bought *The Power of Positive Thinking,* went back to my apartment, and started to read. The book was just what I needed. It methodically turned my focus back to God. As Dr. Peale advocates in the book, I began to meditate on Bible verses such as Isaiah 26:3: *Thou wilt keep him in perfect peace, whose mind is stayed on thee.* I followed the steps Dr. Peale laid out at the end of each chapter. There is no doubt in my mind that the turnaround in attitude I experienced can be traced to the purchase of Dr. Peale's most famous book.

Some months later I moved to New York to study acting and work in the theatre. I found lodging at a rooming house on West 23rd Street, took a job as a temporary typist, volunteered to move scenery at an Off Broadway theatre, and generally fell into the pattern of the city. Which meant a lot of hurrying around and more than a little urban anxiety. At some point I remembered that Dr. Norman Vincent Peale had been a preacher right here in New York. I wondered if he was still alive (this was in the days before the Internet and Google!) I did a little research and found out he'd preached at Marble Collegiate Church. I looked up the address in a phone book and went by to inquire about Dr. Peale. They told me he was not only still alive, but preaching every Sunday, at 82 years of age.

The next Sunday I was there. It was March 9, 1980. I was in the balcony as Dr. Peale delivered his sermon entitled "You Can Win Over All Defeats." I remember being struck how deep and resonant and expressive his voice was. Especially when he said, "The force that is released by faith in Christ is absolutely incredible! There's an invulnerability that flows out of faith. I love that word. *Invulnerability*! And *undefeatable*! That's what you are! You think I'm building you up too much? I do it on the basis of the Bible that says, *This is the victory that overcometh the world*—that means anything *in* the world."

I purchased a tape of the sermon that I still have. On the label is a note I scribbled in ink: *The day I met him*. After the sermon I'd gone to his office, hoping I could shake his hand. A nice secretary said if I'd wait, Dr. Peale would be happy to meet me. I could hear his dynamic voice booming from the office as he spoke to someone on the phone. Presently, Dr. Peale marched out with a smile as his secretary brought him over to me. I introduced myself and he pumped my hand. "Well I am certainly glad to meet *you!*" he said. It struck me immediately that Dr. Peale was the living proof of the value of his philosophy. He had the energy and enthusiasm of a man half his age. When he spoke, he looked me in the eye and for that moment I felt he was treating me as the most important person in the world.

. . .

He asked me what I did, and I said I was a "thespian" and he laughed and said that was *great,* and they could use me at the church. Soon after that they did put me to use. They mounted a Good Friday service and I got to be part of the cast that recreated, in voices from the gallery, the story of the crucifixion. Dr. Peale's preaching continued to encourage me as I pursued my career in New York.

Life took its twists and turns. I got married, moved back to Los Angeles, went to law school, started raising a family. I also began to write. Through those years I'd occasionally re-read Dr. Peale's books and remember fondly his voice resonating from the pulpit of Marble Collegiate Church.

Cut to: this long period of challenge for my wife and me. During those weeks and months we would constantly remind each other to "stay Peale-ish" and pray. It wasn't always easy to be positive, but being Peale-ish got us through many a dark day.

It still does. Whenever I need them, the words of Dr. Norman Vincent Peale are right there waiting for me: "*Invulnerability!* And *undefeatable!* That's what you are!"

Miguel Facusse died. He was 90. The headline of his obit in the *L.A. Times* called him a "colorful, ruthless Honduran tycoon." I had to find out what one of those was, so I read about him. Facusse was a snack mogul. He got educated at Notre Dame here in the good old U. S. of A., then went back to Honduras and started this snack food company and made millions, and with all that money apparently started to throw his weight around. The obit says, "And as Honduras in recent years descended into widespread deadly violence, political chaos and social disaster, Facusse and his security guards were repeatedly accused by human rights groups of responsibility in brutal land grabs and clashes with peasants. Scores of people have been reported killed in the vast Lower Aguan Valley in northeastern Honduras, much of it controlled by Facusse and Dinant." But he had a "folksy demeanor" as if that made all this okay! I say it adds up to ninety wasted years, and now he has gone to meet his Maker, who does not deal in snacks, but in justice. Munch on that, Miguel.

If there is no life after death, this whole dance is absurd. Those who gamble that there isn't any justice beyond the grave are like Benny Southstreet in *Guys and Dolls*. At the Salvation Army meeting, when Nathan Detroit tells him to testify, Benny sheepishly says, "I was always a bad man. I was even a bad gambler. I would like to be a good man, and a good gambler."

People who bet there is no ultimate justice after death are bad gamblers.

~

Evelyn Starks Hardy died. She was 92, and the founder of the Original Gospel Harmonettes, an all-female black singing group that performed in both the Apollo and Carnegie Hall in New York. The Original Gospel Harmonettes were one of the first African-American groups to sign with a major label, and they became a voice for the civil rights movement of the 1960s.

. . .

And what voices! There is nothing quite as soul-stirring as black gospel, and one reason is that it actually believes in the soul, it is rooted in the worship of the God of the Bible, and if you try to take that out of it you will fail, because you can't, which also applies to historians who try to take Christianity out of the civil rights movement, and the Reverend out of the name of Dr. Martin Luther King.

No such nonsense was brooked by Ms. Hardy, who compared the Harmonettes' singing to "The Battle Hymn of the Republic" during the Civil War, which begins *Mine eyes have seen the glory of the coming of the Lord...*

"What that did to the soldiers in the Civil War, our songs did for us in that war [for civil rights]," she once told an interviewer. "It kept us together, it kept us determined to do and to be."

We will get to hear the Harmonettes perform in Heaven, I'm quite sure.

Stan Freberg died. He was 88. He was the father of the funny commercial, an advertising legend. Before he came along most commercials were mere sales copy read by an actor or voiceover guy. Freberg thought you could sell more by making commercials funny. So he proved it. The reason we have commercials like The Most Interesting Man in the World is because Stan Freberg paved the way. He was also a comedian, doing sketches and routines on bestselling comedy albums.

In one campaign, Freberg was tasked with helping Sunsweet prunes. Can you imagine that? Selling prunes? How do you do that? You make it funny. So he got his friend Ray Bradbury to appear in a commercial, setting it in the future with Ray Bradbury on a big screen TV talking to the audience about the virtue of prunes.

Stan Freberg was an outside-the-box thinker, which every culture needs. The Soviet Union didn't have any outside-the-box thinkers. If you thought outside-the-box in the old USSR, they slapped you *into* a box, a cell in the Gulag Archipelago. Aleksandr Solzhenitsyn tried to think outside-the-box. In fact, he tried to think for himself. That got him in Dutch with the Russkies, if you'll pardon the mix. At the time, just after World War II, the USSR was under the thumb of maybe the worst human scum ever to walk the Earth, though there are several scum competing for that title. I'm talking about Josef Stalin, as amoral a monster as there ever was, the soul who may just be the punk that lights the eternal fires of hell. (*Punk,* for you youngsters, is not just a thug or jerk or genre of music, it is also "soft, crumbly wood that has been attacked by fungus, sometimes used as tinder." That is the definition used herein, for Stalin cannot be characterized as a *punk* in the thug sense, since that would be an insult to other thugs).

Every field of endeavor has the pacesetters, the people with the spark and the guts to take risks. Stan Freberg was one of those.

~

Minnie Minoso died. He was 90. He was born in Cuba with the name Saturnino Orestes Armas Miñoso Arrieta, which is not uncommon when you're born in Cuba. At the time they were baseball crazy down there, and still are, and Minnie became the lead in the Cuban-born player boom in the United States. He played for the White Sox and wore number 9, and was one of the most popular players in the city of Chicago, along with Ernie Banks, who also died, as mentioned earlier in this book. Both Minoso and Banks loved to play baseball, probably would have done it for free. Which is how a lot of things ought to be done, for money can often corrupt, as it has sports and politics and show business.

You've just got to have some fun in life, and that's what **Rod "Hot Rod" Hundley** had a lot of. He died at the age of 80, from Alzheimer's, which is a crying shame for a guy with a quick wit and abundant basketball knowledge, which he parlayed on the radio as the announcer for the Jazz basketball franchise. Before that he was a player with the Minneapolis/Los Angeles Lakers. Reporters called him a "showman" because he would do Harlem Globetrottery things even though he was a white guy from West Virginia, and the crowds loved it. He saw basketball as being in great part an entertainment for the fans. He probably inspired a childhood hero of mine, Pete "Pistol Pete" Maravich, one of the greatest basketball players of all time, a guy who could score at will and do things with the basketball that seemed impossible. Think about Earvin "Magic" Johnson. Now imagine Magic doing even more magical things with a basketball. That's when you'll start to get a picture of Pistol Pete Maravich.

. . .

Rod Hundley was an entertainer until he could not entertain anymore.

Ivan Doig died. He was 75. And an author of some acclaim, who I never heard of, which is not a slam on Mr. Doig, or a slam at all, just a fact of life in this age of expanding information and choices, a big bang of info if you will, like the creation of our cosmos when stars and galaxies shot out of nothing at speeds you cannot even calculate in your mind, unless you *are* Stephen Hawking, and even then you might get it wrong because you forgot to carry the two. In any event, Mr. Doig wrote about his native Montana, in fiction and in autobiography, and got good reviews and a following, which is what any author hopes for, and then the author hopes for more, like being on the *New York Times* bestseller list, or in airports in a rack with the cover face out. We are wired that way, to always want more, and part of the art of life is learning how to curb that dog inside you, the envy dog, the never-satisfied dog, because those dogs will chew your curtains and befoul your carpets if you don't train them.

And if you fail to put a lid on those canines, you can end up being a narcissist, which I've run across in my life, and it's a wonder to behold. They call narcissism a "disorder" now, and maybe it really is, instead of just a person deciding each day to be a diva or divo, it's so ingrained in their psyches they can't even recognize it in themselves. Narcissists have a grandiose sense of self-importance, believe they are set apart as special and deserving of high praise and recognition, don't associate with the "little people" but always try to hang out with those of higher status, never do anything wrong (it's always someone else's fault), fantasize that critics are merely envious of their superior achievements (when in fact they are envious of others but don't recognize it); have no empathy at all (like a sociopath), and are generally a pill to be around ("Enough about me. What do *you* think of my books?")

Homaro Cantu died, and he was but 38, an apparent suicide, though my thriller-author sense is pressed to ask questions, because Mr. Cantu was found hanging at a brewery he was building, and his wife said he did not leave a note and had no history of mental illness or depression, and indeed was on top of his world as a renowned chef in Chicago at a restaurant called Moto and, says the NYT obit, "was among a small vanguard of American chefs who used chemical-laboratory techniques to coax food into novel and sometimes peculiar forms."

He once served "synthetic champagne" by squirting it into a glass with a large medical syringe. He made paper taste like food. People spent up to $240 for his twenty-course meals.

Nice work if you can get it. But Mr. Cantu was serious, as he dreamed of his edible paper being an answer to the world's starvation problem.

The only problem reported by the obit was that a month before his death an investor in Moto sued Mr. Cantu because he'd never received any share of the profits, and also accused the chef of misuse of funds.

. . .

So it is conceivable that the suicide had something to do with this lawsuit, and that is unfortunate, as is any suicide, except those of Adolf Hitler and Herman Goering.

Socrates was pressed into his own demise for the sin of "corrupting the youth of Athens," meaning teaching them to think and question authority. All the old teacher did was go around asking pointed questions that got to the heart of things, shook up assumptions, and boy can we use that now in this unthinking age when the deepest reflections one has are what kind of nosh to procure at the food court in the mall.

Pauline Wiggin died. She was 97, and the mother of a writer friend of mine, Eric Wiggin. She was born on May 20, 1918 in North Palermo, Maine, at the home of her grandparents. That's the way it was a lot in those days, families all living under the same roof, not as transient as we are today, movers and shakers (especially in California) are we, restless and weary, fast and distracted, tone deaf to the rhythms of nature because our ears have noise in them, pumped from iPods or smart phones (which are not really smart at all, but products of design, thus it is the designer who is intelligent and smart, which applies to the universe, too).

Pauline grew up on a farm, which was also common in those days. We've flipped the balance, it used to be farms mostly and a few cities. Now it's big cities and a few farms. Pauline got married in 1938 and had seven children, and she was a church-going woman all her life and served wherever she was planted. A nice, full life of 97 years.

My grandfather was born on a farm in 1890. He had a deep, resonant laugh. I can hear it still. In his lifetime Lindbergh flew the Atlantic, Babe Ruth hit 60 home runs in a season, FDR was elected four times, the Kaiser was defeated, Hitler was defeated, JFK was assassinated, and the Beatles arrived in America.

Be aware, look around, experience, analyze, enjoy, argue (with facts and logic), and try to develop a deep, resonant laugh.

Paul Almond died. He was 83. A film and TV director, he worked with a lot of stars before they got really famous, like Sean Connery and William Shatner. But the best thing he ever did, in my view, was a film called *Seven Up!* which was a documentary shown on BBC TV in 1964. In this a group of seven-year-old children in Britain were interviewed and followed around, chronicling their hopes and dreams. It was funny and touching, but the real genius of this project was that every seven years these same kids were interviewed, to see how they were doing. It has followed them all the way up to age 56! Almond only directed the first one, then Michael Apted took over, but Almond was there at the beginning, and in that first film there was a little boy named Tony who had the childhood dream of becoming a jockey ... and ended up as a taxi driver.

· · ·

I can relate. When I was a kid I went through a horse phase, where I wanted to ride them, like Roy Rogers and Randolph Scott, and then I saw National Velvet with Elizabeth Taylor and Mickey Rooney, and thought being a jockey was the way to go. So I went to my mom and said, "I want to be a jockey." At that time I was sprouting into what would eventually become a nearly 6'4" basketball player, and my mom smiled understandingly and said, "But honey, jockeys have to be short. And you're not going to be short."

"Why not?"

"Because your uncle is six-seven. And you're already tall for your age."

"But that's not fair," I said, because I'd been told you can become anything you want in America, even President of the United States, and I never heard there was a jockey exception!

But alas, another lesson of life was being handed to me, that old chestnut "life is unfair." And that was a real bummer to hear, because we want life to be fair, for everybody, and we don't want people to cheat, but people do cheat, and gain advantage, so you're tempted to cheat, and that's what's happening in schools because every kid wants to get into Harvard or Stanford and make a lot of money, which is a terrible way to look at the life of the university, which used to be about learning the great wisdom of the ages so you could best get along in a life that may not be fair, and do so without cheating.

.   .   .

So I didn't become a jockey. I went to baseball, then basketball, then into acting, then became a lawyer, then a writer, and all along the way I did what my dad told me to do—work hard and play fair—and it's worked out pretty well for me, all things considered.

William Price Fox died at the age of 89, and I'm sorry to say I didn't know of him, sorry because he was a fellow author and apparently one who garnered a lot of praise for his work, which was of the Southern variety, which is why I didn't know about him, not being much of a reader of Southern fiction, not out of any Yankee animosity but simply because, leaving *To Kill a Mockingbird* out of the discussion, I've just never really connected with it. Perhaps that has to do with me never liking Faulkner. I had to read Faulkner in college and I just did not get him, and I still don't, which is likely more a reflection on me than on Mr. Faulkner, but it just took too much effort and even after the effort I wasn't really satisfied that the effort was worth it, not when there was Hemingway and Steinbeck out there, and Saroyan and even Scott Fitzgerald, but most of all Hammett and Chandler. If I could redesign every high school reading list across this great country of ours I would make sure *The Maltese Falcon* was on that list, even if I had to nudge out *The Great Gatsby* to do it. For while I admire *Gatsby,* it's from a distance, and it doesn't turn boys into readers, which is what we need to have happen more in high school, nor does it even tell us as much about humanity than does *Falcon.*

.   .   .

And then I'd put *Farewell, My Lovely* on that reading list, too, so we'd have two hard-boiled books, which we need to balance all the soft-boiled material on high school reading lists, and then we'd need teachers who knew what they were talking about when they taught these books, and that is perhaps a far greater concern at this point, the art of teaching having fallen into such disarray and dismemberment at the behest of committees who are beholden to political pressures, to the point of holding up lesser works of art because they contain some preferred agenda or political view, which should be a subject for social studies or history, not a lit class.

Which is all to say, it's no surprise to me that I missed out on Mr. Fox's literary accomplishments, but it is something I will try to remedy, for he also wrote essays and articles in addition to his novels, and so do I, and that makes me interested, as does this clip from an essay he wrote on chitlins, which come from the intestines of a hog:

The chitlin, a long tubelike affair, is stretched out and scraped down, then turned inside out and scraped again. Three lengths are braided together, boiled until tender, then battered, deep-fried and served. And who will eat a chitlin? Max Gergel, a Columbia sage I travel with and who is famous for promoting the now-defunct insecticide "Sam Chewning's Roach's Last Supper" (featuring a four-color label of 12 roaches chowing down at the da Vinci table) explained: "You take a man and tie him to a stake and feed him bread and water and nothing else for seven days and seven nights, and then he will eat a chitlin." Max, who can stretch and roll a sentence out until it sounds like it was lifted from

Ecclesiastes, paused carefully. "He won't like it, but he will eat it."

That's a fine passage in and of itself, and the subject of the essay is perfect, for the true art of this form of literature is to take something seemingly mundane and make it come alive. Two authors who could do this regularly are Joseph Epstein and **William Zinsser**, who died on May 12, 2015 at the age of 92.

Mr. Zinsser's name is known to countless writers, for he is the author of *On Writing Well,* a book that has become a bona fide classic for non-fiction authors of all stripes (a good old-fashioned phrase, *of all stripes.* But how many know it is derived from the art of weaving? How many know what *warp and woof* means? How many would guess it means something Scooby Doo would say?).

I got to meet William Zinsser when I was on a trip to New York with my wife. He had consented to see us at his Upper East Side digs. In fact, he told me that we were the first "guinea pigs" in this latest phase of his life. Glaucoma had forced William Zinsser, then age 89, to finally cease his prodigious output of the written word. He had decided now to concentrate on his role as a mentor and encourager of writers, to help them in any way he can. "I'm still working out how that will look," he said.

So we sat and talked. About writing and his career. He is a fourth generation New Yorker. He's always lived in the city, not counting a stint in North Africa and Italy during WWII, and in

New Haven when he taught at Yale. After the war, he "cadged" a job at the newspaper he grew up with, the *New York Herald-Tribune*. It was here he learned the lessons on writing he would live by and pass on. As to the facts: Get it right. As to style: Second best is no good.

He did his work on a classic Underwood typewriter. "I'm a child of paper," he told me. "And that Underwood is still in my closet."

Zinsser loved working on the newspaper, but saw it sadly decline in the late fifties due to mismanagement. When he couldn't take it anymore he quit and became a freelance writer. This was quite a switch, from regular paycheck to the uncertainty and fickleness of the freelance life.

It didn't faze him. "You have to make your own luck," he said. "No one's going to do it for you."

So he wrote for the top magazines—*Life, Look, The Saturday Evening Post*—until they died. He made more of his own luck by turning to teaching—at Yale and later at the Columbia School of Journalism and the New School.

He finally put his words of writing wisdom into *On Writing Well*, which doesn't sound like the title of a blockbuster. But, 1.5 million copies later, it certainly qualifies.

·   ·   ·

I would also highly recommend Mr. Zinsser's book about his own writing journey, *Writing Places*. It is one of the most enjoyable memoirs I've ever read.

But my absolute favorite Zinsser piece is a little gem of cultural history, *Writing With a Word Processor*. Published in 1983, it is the account of his transition from typewriter to computer. It still makes me laugh. Even though the technology aspect is dated, the writing remains fresh, clear and hilarious. I'll sometimes take it off the shelf and read a random chapter to my wife, and we'll laugh again at how he captured that historical and hysterical slice of life.

When our chat was over and we were about to leave, Mr. Zinsser reflected on the new technologies available for the writer these days. They are about convenience, but not essence, he said. They don't fundamentally change what writing has always been about.

"We are all in the storytelling business," he said, "whatever the technology you're set up with. Most of what I've done, frankly, is tell a story."

Joanne Carson died. She was 83. The obituary in the *Los Angeles Daily News* gave her this headline: *Ex-wife of Former Tonight Show host Johnny Carson*. Now that's a heck of a thing to be long remembered for. She married Carson in 1963, right after he started hosting the show. They divorced in 1973, a matter which Carson joked about for years, mostly about all the money he had to give up because of it. Meanwhile, she had a second marriage later in her life, to a fellow named Richard Revere, which invites the question (not *begs the question* which people think means the same thing, but doesn't, because *begs the question* is a *fallacy of logic,* which means someone has not answered the question, they have in fact assumed an answer without support. So the next time you say *"That begs the question..."* in conversation, I want you to hear my voice in your head and I want it to make you stutter and say, *"I mean, I'm sorry, I meant to say that invites the question..."* and when you hear a news talking head say *"That begs the question..."* I want you to think, *That's not what it means...* And speaking further of things that shouldn't be said, I want you to throw something at the screen whenever a politician or pundit says *"At the end of the day..."* I'm sorry, I've been waiting for that day to end for years now, so that cliché won't be spouted anymore. Can we have some original thinking again? Please? But I digress) why wasn't Joanne Carson known in her obit as Joanne Revere? Did she make that choice herself? But why would she do that, being divorced from Johnny Carson, who everyone ought to agree was the greatest at his profession, a profession he practically invented, though some will point to Jack Paar or Steve Allen, both of whom should be pointed to for their contribution to talk show history. But no one did it better than Carson, who never lost his Nebraska decency in the way he treated guests. It was his easy charm and ability to ask real questions and be funny at the same time, but never so as to bring shame or derision on a guest, even when poking fun, because you knew he wasn't being mean about it, and was able to take a good-natured joke himself, as was oft delivered by his sidekick, Ed McMahon, who elevated the role of sidekick into a major gig which not many people can pull off, which is why there aren't many "second bananas" anymore, though I would call out Andy Richter who does a great job for Conan O'Brien.

. . .

One interesting fact about Joanne Carson was that she became a close friend of the writer Truman Capote (who was born Truman Streckfus Persons) and though the obit didn't mention how they met, I'm sure it was because Capote was often a guest on *The Tonight Show* where he did, frankly, the best Truman Capote impression I've ever seen (Phillip Seymour Hoffman is a close second). I say impression, because I do think Capote never was solidly himself, was always in a persona, always searching for a self and a belonging. I recall talking to a publicity person from a major publishing house who once had to squire Capote to a book signing and interview in a major city. It was morning and she was in the limo and Capote had one demand, that the limo have a couple of bottles of vodka, and immediately upon entering the limo he grabbed a large glass and threw in some ice cubes and filled the glass with vodka and didn't bother with tomato juice or anything else. A sad state of affairs, and Capote was certainly not the only author to be ruined by booze, but in any event he needed friends and Joanne was one of them, and she kept a writing room for him at her house, which was very large because of the Carson divorce decree, and in fact this is where Truman Capote died at the age of 59.

Capote was cremated and Joanne Carson kept half his ashes, the other half going to Capote's longtime companion, Jack Dunphy. But rest in peace Capote did not, for on Halloween night in 1988, during a party at Joanne Carson's home, somebody stole Capote's ashes and also $200,000 worth of jewelry, though the thief was thoughtful enough to return the ashes, leaving the urn near the garden hose at Joanne Carson's house. Joanne purchased a crypt for the ashes at Westwood Memorial, and that is where half of Truman Capote now resides, locked up near some of his friends, including Marilyn Monroe and Natalie Wood and Mel Tormé, who was one of the great jazz singers of all time with perhaps the greatest of all nicknames, The Velvet Fog.

Speaking of Marilyn Monroe—and in the 1950s men spoke of little else—for years and years a rose was placed daily in the vase at Monroe's crypt, paid for by her ex-husband Joe DiMaggio. That was quite a pairing back in the day, DiMaggio being a national sports icon and Monroe the reigning sex symbol of the silver screen. She exuded such sexual ferocity that she was not taken seriously as an actress, which is too bad because she did develop some acting chops, which you can see on display in movies like *Bus Stop* and *The Misfits* and maybe best of all *Some Like It Hot*, which was a comedy, but to play comedy right you have to be a good actor, and she did it right in that movie, her timing was perfect, her delivery sublime. As was Jack Lemmon's when he delivered an immortal line. In the film Lemmon and Tony Curtis play musicians in the 1920s who witness a gangland killing, and have to go on the run. In drag, they get hired on to be part of an all-girl band, Sweet Sue And Her Society Syncopators. As they show up at the train station to take off, they see, walking in front of them, Sugar Kane (Monroe) whose caboose has a jiggle that cannot be ignored. Lemmon says, "Look at that! Look how she moves. It's just like Jell-O on springs!"

But Marilyn was to become a tragic figure, dying under question-able circumstances in 1962, the official cause being suicide via barbiturate poisoning. But there have been all sorts of conspiracy theories about her death, some of which include President John F. Kennedy, who reportedly bedded Monroe, which wouldn't be a surprise because he bedded scores of women, which isn't exactly a good character reference. But JFK was assassinated, he was elevated to secular sainthood, because that's what happens with death, there is a moment when you wonder how a person shall be remembered, and things have to break just the right way to be remembered well, even if your life wasn't all that much to speak of when you were alive. Like James Dean, a fine young actor, but he only made three movies and then drove too fast up around Paso Robles and crashed and died, and then became a great acting icon which was a little higher than he deserved, for he was a bit of a scenery chewer.

Then there are those who have a seemingly good life but something goes terribly wrong, and it stains them, and for the rest of their days they fight back trying to recover their reputations, like Dan Rather, who went after George W. Bush as he was running for re-election in 1984, and got carried away by some fraudulent documents that purportedly cast a bad light on the prez, and yet even when those docs were shown to be suspect Mr. Rather kept sticking with them, and that came back to bite him in the journalistic butt and he was fired by CBS and he's barely been heard of since, except when he was played by Robert Redford in a movie that flopped. Rather's entire career now has a coffee stain on it, for this incident will appear in anything henceforth written about him, including his obituary.

And so it goes, and the only thing you can do is adopt a set of values that you have thought through and that you honor in your living, so that when you die it is with the knowledge that you did your best by your lights and you have nothing to be ashamed of, except maybe some youthful indiscretions or uncharacteristic errors of judgment, and thus the overall trend line of your life is upward.

~

B. B. King died. He was 89. The King of the Blues could get that electric guitar of his to weep, and the deep resonance of his voice plucked the listener's soul. He did what he did for a long time, performing up to 250 times a year in his prime. That's a good artistic life, being able to do what you love to do in front of audiences who appreciate the artistry. He was the opposite of Emily Dickinson, who wrote her poems in a lonely room in Amherst, Massachusetts, most of which were not published until after her death. But I wonder if there was any difference in the heart, when B. B. sang the blues and Emily wrote of love and death. I suspect they both, in their best moments, were one with their songs, everything else shut out for that moment, the artistic moment, it's both expression and escape, it's a falling in and a letting go.

Which is also the way to describe extreme sports, especially BASE jumping—that stands for Buildings, Antennas, Spans (bridges), and Earth (cliffs). **Dean Potter** was a BASE jumper, who died at the age of 43 when he donned a "wingsuit" and tried to fly over Yosemite Park. He didn't make it. It was just a matter of time, so they said, because Dean Potter challenged death all the time.

"BASE jumping is the most dangerous thing you can do," his friend said. "The odds are not in your favor, and sadly Dean pulled the unlucky card."

. . .

So does that mean you shouldn't play this game? We all choose what we want to play, and the Dean Potters of the world don't find any value in a game that doesn't have a death-defying vibe to it.

You don't need physical death to make a game worth playing. You can take risks that aren't a danger to your bones. That's the sweet spot of achievers and artists, getting into a risk zone and going for something. But if you fail, you know you are stronger and can get up again. A BASE jumper who fails doesn't get up again.

Johnny Strange was killed at the age of 23. He also crashed wearing a wingsuit in the Swiss Alps. He crashed a few seconds after taking off from Mt. Gitschen.

Someone who knew him said, "He lived more in twenty-three years than many do their whole life."

Life is a gift and you can play with it, blow it, extol it, share it, mess it up, make it shine. It's sad when someone young goes for the kick and gets given the boot. Only old people should die.

Yes, **Anne Meara** was old by conventional measures, 85, but she was young in that wonderfully comedic mind she had all her life. She was, of course, one half of the great comedy team of Stiller & Meara, who in the 1960s consistently appeared on the Ed Sullivan show, which in those days was like getting a guest shot in Heaven, with everybody on Earth tuning in, and Ed standing in the wings like God, which he was of his show, and it's hard for youngsters today to wrap their heads around someone like Ed Sullivan, back in the days when there were only three networks, so your viewing choices were limited, you couldn't go to YouTube on your phone or Hulu on your tablet, and you had to get up and walk to the TV to turn a dial, and on Sunday nights most people in America who were watching the tube watched Ed Sullivan, and by the way every voice impressionist had an Ed Sullivan imitation, because he was so easy to do, and it was always funny (George Carlin once said that even a bear could do Ed Sullivan), and I had a killer Sullivan myself, I'd put my shoulders up and do the voice and here was the real secret to doing a good Ed Sullivan: you had to make up the most outrageous acts. See, Ed Sullivan would introduce every act on his stage—from The Beatles to Stiller & Meara to Topo Gigio, the Italian mouse puppet. So in my Ed Sullivan impression I'd say, "Tonight on our show (by the way, Ed tended to flatten the word *show* so it sometime sounded like *shoe,* so when you hear some old fart on the radio joking about a "really big shoe" that's from Ed Sullivan) we have the entire female population of Guadalajara singing the hits of Kate Smith..." and so on. I love doing Sullivan, but you can't anymore, because if the person is under fifty they'll just look at you like you're having a seizure, and that's a shame, because Ed Sullivan imitations should be forever. Now you kids, if you want to know your cultural history, and Ed Sullivan intrigues you, then watch the movie *Bye Bye Birdie* sometime, because that captures the Sullivan aura, and Ed plays himself, and this family hears that it's going to be on the Ed Sullivan show because their daughter has won a contest to get to kiss Conrad Birdie (an Elvis knockoff) before Conrad goes into the Army.

The daughter is played by Ann-Margret who was an absolute dish, as they used to say.

Which brings me back to Anne Meara, who was the mother of Ben Stiller, and the wife of Jerry, who most people know as Frank Costanza on *Seinfeld* or Arthur Spooner on *The King of Queens*. Anne was an Irish Catholic from Brooklyn and Jerry was a Jewish kid from the same burg, and eventually they turned those backgrounds into comedy bits and 36 appearances on Sullivan.

They stayed married to each other, which is something magnificent in show business, so hats off to Anne Meara and Jerry Stiller, and a tip of the shoulders to Ed Sullivan for making them popular.

Omar Sharif died. He was 83. He had one of the greatest acting entrances of all time, in his film debut in *Lawrence of Arabia*. You have to see it on the big screen to appreciate it, for it is a David Lean film, all of which are meant to be seen on the biggest screens possible, for the visual artistry of them, the physical sweep, all done in the days before CG, which is kind of cheating in the movies, and this film was shot in the actual desert and at one point Lawrence, played by Peter O'Toole, is relaxing at a well with his guide when way, way off in the distance a tiny, tiny black dot appears. You could not see this dot if you watched *Lawrence of Arabia* on a small black and white TV, as I once did when I was a student at the University of California, Santa Barbara, and had a six-inch portable TV in the dorm, and I'm sure poor David Lean would have had cardiac arrest had he happened to be walking by the room with my door open and heard the soundtrack by the great Maurice Jarre and stopped to see where it was coming from and it was coming from a tiny box that only showed pictures in black and white. So I'm very glad the great Lean was not in Santa Rosa Hall that particular evening, but still there was the dot, and on the big screen in full color the dot took a whole lot of screen time to get bigger and bigger, it seemed like ten minutes, until it got close—and shot and killed the guide for drinking from the wrong well!—and then finally appeared as a black-clad, camel-riding son of the desert. The camel drops to its knees and off he slips, and it is Omar Sharif, who gave a commanding performance that earned him a Supporting Actor nod.

His most famous role was another one for Lean, as the titular poet in *Dr. Zhivago.* Here his love interest was Julie Christie, and quite a love interest she was, too. This film has some of the most magnificent cinematography ever, as does the later Lean film *Ryan's Daughter,* but that movie was something of a flop, and may just be the most magnificent mediocre film ever made, by which I mean a small story that was stretched onto a huge canvas, and it doesn't quite make it, though the delight is an against-type performance by Robert Mitchum, who quietly steals the movie along with that cagey old actor Trevor Howard as the grizzled parish priest.

Omar also played Nicky Arnstein in *Funny Girl,* and worked steadily after that, but his real passion was playing Bridge, and he used to do that indoors while smoking several of his one-hundred-a-day Egyptian cigarettes, which are serious cigarettes, and which accounted for his appearance late in life, like a cast member of

The Walking Dead (and I don't mean the humans). But the man had some kind of iron constitution, for he did make it to 83, and then his heart decided enough was enough.

~

Kenny "The Snake" Stabler died. He was 69. Back in a day when pro football players were not part machine, built of trainers and diet and sometimes enhancing drugs, there were players who played because they were good on the field but also because the money they earned let them live the way they wanted to live off the field, which made them "colorful." Such was Ken Stabler, a left-handed quarterback for the Oakland Raiders when the Raiders were actually a good team, coached by the great John Madden, and Stabler was their leader who led them to a Super Bowl win, but when not on the field he would be off drinking and smoking and sometimes drugging (not the performance enhancing kind, but the nose-candy kind) and womanizing, and driving fast cars and boats, because some people are like that, they have an inner engine that doesn't turn off, and when you're in your twenties or early thirties maybe you can do that for a while, but pretty soon your body looks at you and says, "Really?" and starts to shut itself down in various ways, and that's what happened to Stabler, who had about five good years as a QB and then went down and eventually out of football. But when he played, he was as wily as a snake, and he always found a way to win.

~

E. L. Doctorow died. He was 84. He was a famous American writer, won all kinds of literary awards, and had this great metaphor about writing. He said writing fiction was like driving on a highway at night with your headlights on. What he meant was that you can only see as far as the lights will go, then you drive to that spot, then you see where to drive next.

It's one of those metaphors that writers of fiction love to talk about and debate, sort of like the men who gather together in veteran's halls across the land and argue about war and hippies. The debate among writers is this: is it better to map out a whole story before you start writing? Or should you just go where your wonderful wild writer's mind leads you, moment by moment, and see where you end up?

As I stated earlier in this book, there is a perceived difference between being a "plotter" and a "pantser." The plotters are those who like to plan things out before they start to write. They make outlines, sometimes huge. Like a fellow named James Patterson, who has had some success. The kid may break out soon. But he is known for copious outlines, some of which are given to his co-writers for the actual writing.

On the other side of the fence are people like Stephen King, who claims that all you have to do is come up with a great situation and characters and then let things ride, and eventually you'll figure out an ending. I hope I am not too cheeky in pointing out that though I think Stephen King is one of the most gifted writers we've ever seen, sometimes his endings don't quite make it, there is a feeling that he had written himself into a corner and gotten out of it with something huge or gross to distract us.

.   .   .

Then there are those who are somewhere in between. Isaac Asimov used to say he had a beginning and an ending, and then let himself have the fun of figuring out how to get there in his E. L. Doctorow-powered automobile (he actually didn't say that about the Doctorow car, I don't know if he even knew Doctorow, though he probably read *Ragtime* like everybody else did back in 1975, and a bunch of the same people saw the movie which, for me, is best known because it brought the great James Cagney out of retirement to play one memorable scene as a New York police commissioner facing off with the black piano player turned militant, Coalhouse Walker. About all I remember from the movie, in fact, is that Cagney voice yelling, "Walker!")

Writers enjoy these debates. I have been studying the craft of writing since 1988 and I've written a few books about it myself, one of which remains, much to my delight, something of a bible for writers. It's called *Plot & Structure*, and no I don't claim to be the Moses of the writing set coming down from Sinai with the laws of fiction, but I am gratified to hear from writers almost every week telling me how much the book has meant to them.

That, I think, is what writers love to hear most and strive to achieve. Whether it's fiction or nonfiction, having a reader say a book moved them, made them cry, made them laugh, entertained them, outraged them (in a good way, not because the writing stunk, thank you), instructed them, that is like the Balm of Gilead to a writer. It's even better than money, though I'm not ashamed to say that writing for money is an absolutely legitimate thing to do, to make a living, to take care of a family, so long as one is not selling one's soul in order to do it. There are certain things I could write that would make me a lot of money but I won't write because I have to look at myself in the mirror when I shave. My image in the mirror would look back at me and shake its head in disdain like in some episode of *Twilight Zone* where I have to confront my true inner self. I do not want to hear Rod Serling in the next room, cigarette in hand, saying "Mr. James Scott Bell, who fancied himself a writer, but who made a deal with the devil when he wrote something purely for money, and when it rolled in started writing more of the same. Mr. James Scott Bell, who at one time wanted to be America's best writer, now consigned to the remainder section of the Twilight Zone."

E. L. Doctorow, on the other hand, wrote in that zone between literary and commercial that is inhabited by very few, where critics laud and readers buy, and perhaps he was a literary genius. That's something that will get you places, writing places I mean, having literary genius, although it's not a guarantee. I have known some people who are geniuses in that regard and never quite made it because they think genius is enough. Genius is not enough. Genius has to be put through the boot camp of craft and hard work, so you can't just think that your brain, a gift of God by the way, is going to sit there on autopilot and make you a fortune. Your genius needs a drill sergeant who says, "You think you know what you're doing, don't you? You get down and give me twenty, maggot, you give me twenty and every time you come up I want you to scream *I will keep my point of view consistent in every scene, Sir!*"

A nature lover committed to bird conservation named **Wes Craven** died. He was 76. He was also a director of horror movies, most famously *A Nightmare on Elm Street*. Which just goes to show that you never know what's underneath the surface of a person—the old "You can't tell a book by its cover" routine, though sometimes you can make a pretty good guess about a book by its cover, meaning if you have a shirtless male with six-pack abs on the front, tight jeans with the button popped, it's probably a good guess that you've got some kind of romance thing here, and it will deliver its goods (if I may be so bold) in a certain form and fashion, meaning the woman who dares to fall for the alpha male, and the alpha male who finds the one woman who can tame him, will end up together at the end.

There is romance and there is erotica, and there is now a genre called "dark erotica," which was spawned by the runaway success of a book called *Fifty Shades of Grey,* which is about the romantic side of abusing women. This dark erotica is defined as: *Sexy and sensual. Unlike Erotic Romance, Dark Erotica features an unconventional love story with an anti-hero and may not have a happy ending. The stories in this category can be suspenseful or even psychologically thrilling, and many of them explore the forbidden or taboo. Some common tropes found in Dark Erotica include the mafia, kidnapping, captor/captive, blackmail/coercion, abuse, and nonconsensual sex.*

I can remember a time when kids just went to the soda shop. Glad to see that things have progressed, which is why everyone is so happy these days.

Yvonne Craig died. She was 78. And she was not supposed to die, for she was the original Batgirl on the old *Batman* TV show with Adam West. That made her a pioneer of female superheroes onscreen, especially of the type that fills a tight superhero suit in a most pleasing manner.

She worked steadily in television until the roles dried up, but kept going to appearances for fans of the show. In other words, she was remembered fondly, and isn't that a nice thing to have in life? **Martin Milner** had a life like that. He died at the age of 83. He started as a child actor and then went on to a great television career, getting starring roles in two iconic series. The second of these was *Adam-12*, a drama about LAPD patrol officers. Milner and his partner, played by Kent McCord, would patrol the streets of Los Angeles, and it was all filmed on location.

But Milner's coolest role was as Todd Stiles in *Route 66,* which was cool because it had the coolest of all musical themes, written by Nelson Riddle, and the coolest of all cars, a Corvette, and the coolest of concepts—Todd would drive around the country in a boss Corvette and stop places and find pretty girls and trouble that he had to fight his way out of. Todd had a friend named Buzz, played by George Maharis, who was a tough guy from a rough background, so they were always getting into scrapes but also showed their hearts by helping victims get justice.

Being free on the open road is a standard male fantasy. There was another series I remember as a kid called *Then Came Bronson,* starring Michael Parks, who played a guy named Bronson (how's that for a coincidence?), who left the so-called rat race and just got on a motorcycle and drove around the country, finding pretty girls and getting into trouble. At the beginning of the series it shows Bronson in traffic next to a guy in a car who looks like the typical working stiff of the day. He's tired, his hat is tilted back on his head, and he looks at Bronson and asks him if he's going on a trip. Bronson says he is. The guy asks him where he's going, and Bronson says,

"Wherever I end up, I guess." The guy heaves a big sigh and says, "Man, I wish I was you."

Every working stiff feels this way from time to time, wishing he could get out of the routine and be free, not have any responsibilities, even if those responsibilities include the wife and kiddies. The real men, the good men, may entertain the fantasy, but they don't leave the wife and kiddies, because they know that commitment is a sacrifice, and that sacrifice is part of the good life, oddly enough—more rich and heroic than a life of a man-child who just does whatever he wants, even on a motorcycle or in a Corvette.

Martin Milner himself was that kind of hero, staying married to the same woman for 58 years, which is getting close to the Hollywood record, and fathering four children. Martin Milner could have taken his TV money and run off to an island with any number of the beautiful actresses who got guest roles on *Route 66*. But he didn't. And that's the point.

Dickie Moore died at 89. He was a child actor and had a long career in Hollywood. He is best known as the first boy to give a screen kiss to Shirley Temple, when she was fourteen, in a movie called *Little Annie Rooney*. I guess that's something because not many of us get to be *the first* at something. I've been the first a couple of times. I was the first writer to have a self-published work nominated for an International Thriller Writers Award, for my novella *One More Lie*. I'm kind of proud of that. I was the first suspense writer to win a Christy Award, too, which was just a matter of timing. They'd just decided to start an award for Christian fiction and unbeknownst to me my publisher at the time nominated my novel *Final Witness* and it won. A lot of life is about timing over which you have no control. Sometimes the timing is good, sometimes bad, and that's the way life rolls and you have to roll with it, and set yourself up to be ready the next time.

Dickie Moore was also the deaf boy in the film noir classic *Out of the Past*, starring Robert Mitchum and Kirk Douglas. Many people consider this to be the quintessential noir, and it is very close to that, in great part because it has a femme fatale played by Jane Greer, who is supposed to be so hubba hubba, so alluring, that men would risk death in order to possess her. I have nothing against Jane Greer, she was a fine actress, but that role should have been played by the actress who is in another part of the film, that actress being Rhonda Fleming. Fleming was not yet a big star, but she became one, and I'm telling you the hubba hubba factor is off the charts with Rhonda Fleming, and I would have believed that men would risk death to possess her. She had red hair and a figure that would make a bishop kick out a stained glass window (that last line borrowed from Raymond Chandler, who gave us a lot of great lines, including *The coffee shop smell was strong enough to build a garage on*.)

When you line up all the child stars over the years, the majority of them have not fared well after they grew up. Shirley Temple turned out all right, was even our ambassador to the United Nations for a while, so good for her. Dickie Moore went into public relations and had a successful career, so good for him.

But Carl Switzer, who played Alfalfa in the old *Little Rascals* shorts, grew up and fought a guy over a $50 debt, and pulled a knife on the fellow. The fellow then shot Switzer in the groin, causing massive bleeding that led to his death. Carl "Alfalfa" Switzer couldn't even catch a break on timing, for he died the same day as legendary Hollywood director Cecil B. DeMille, who got all the press coverage in the papers.

This is the part of life that brings sadness, which is in a pan on one side of the scales, with joy in the other pan. This is the Cliff's Notes summary of the Book of Ecclesiastes, which everyone should read in order to understand life, the universe, and everything.

Jackie Collins died at age 77. She was a prolific novelist who sold hundreds of millions of books, mainly because she happily wrote plots about explicit sexual escapades, and of course "sex sells" as the aforementioned *Fifty Shades of Grey* has shown. Jackie Collins was the original *Fifty Shades* lady, though in those days you couldn't be quite so, um, descriptive. She was also the sister of the actress Joan Collins, who was once hot and heavy with Warren Beatty, but then it's only three or four degrees of separation between you and someone who was hot and heavy with Warren Beatty, but even for men like Warren eventually the car won't make it up the hill like it used to. I'm glad Beatty settled down with one wife, Annette Bening.

Warren Beatty, by the way, is the brother of the actress Shirley MacLaine, who was incredibly cute and desirable in the move *The Apartment,* co-starring Jack Lemmon and Fred MacMurray. Interestingly, MacMurray was everyone's favorite dad on a TV show called *My Three Sons,* but his greatest roles in film were as crumbs.

Think about *Double Indemnity.* He plays a slick talking insurance man who teams up with a dame to knock off her husband. A murderer! Yet, by the middle of the film, we find ourselves pulling for him. I don't know many actors who could make that happen.

And I don't think, outside of Robert Mitchum, there's ever been a better deliverer of rat-a-tat film noir lines, like these:

"That's a honey of an anklet you're wearing."

"How could I have known that murder can sometimes smell like honeysuckle?"

"I wonder if a little rum would get this up on its feet."

. . .

Inexplicably, MacMurray was never nominated for an Academy Award. Outrage! He was absolutely robbed when Barry Fitzgerald was somehow nominated for Best Supporting Actor and Best Actor *for the same role* (*Going My Way*). MacMurray should have been given the Actor slot for *Double Indemnity* (Fitzgerald won for Support). Bing Crosby won Actor that year (again, for *Going My Way*) and while the old crooner was fine, he didn't do one tenth the acting MacMurray does in *Double Indemnity*.

MacMurray also played crumbs in *The Caine Mutiny* and *The Apartment*. He should have won a supporting Oscar for at least one of those.

In other words, he was a true actor, doing his job and doing it well. He never tried to show off or chew scenery. He blended into the role and served the greater purpose of the movie. That's not a bad way to do any job, is it?

The great Yankee ballplayer **Yogi Berra** died at age 90. He was a Hall of Fame catcher, a three time MVP, and his most famous play was during the 1955 World Series when Jackie Robinson stole home. The ump called Robinson safe and Yogi went crazy, and to this day you can look at the film in slo-mo and make an argument either way, though it seems to favor the Yogi side if you want my own opinion, and even if you don't.

.   .   .

He was built like a catcher, 5'8" and pudgy. His face was nothing to write home about, and Yankee GM Larry McPhail reflected that Yogi looked like the "bottom man on an unemployed acrobatic team." But this squat, goofy-looking backstop played on ten—count 'em—ten World Series championship teams.

As storied as Yogi's baseball career was, he is most famous for uttering things that, on the surface, seem odd and contradictory, yet on second glance make some sort of bizarre sense, at least to Yogi himself. The start of all that, according to Yogi, was when the Yankees threw a Yogi Berra Day in 1947, and Yogi took to the microphone to thank the brass and the fans, and said, "Thank you for making this day necessary."

From then on, it was one golden nugget after another. Like when a restaurant in his home town of St. Louis got popular. "Nobody goes there anymore," Yogi said. "It's too crowded."

Of baseball: "Ninety percent of the game is half mental."

Of money: "A nickel ain't worth a dime anymore."

Of life: "When you come to a fork in the road, take it."

Exactly!

Kevin Corcoran died at the age of 66, but I can never see him as anything but ten. That was how old he was when he made *Toby Tyler,* the Disney movie about a boy who ran away to join the circus. I was about seven when I saw it, and immediately decided I was going to do the same thing. The fact that *Toby Tyler* takes place during the early 1900s in the Midwest did not dissuade a boy living in a Los Angeles suburb during the Kennedy administration.

I even made myself a bindle stick out of an old broom handle and a kerchief. I wanted to run away with the right look.

I put the bindle on my shoulder and set off. When I got to the corner of my block, a man who lived across the street asked me where I was going. I said, "I'm running away." He yelled, "You get home!"

I turned around and sheepishly went home.

See, in those days, neighbors looked out for each other, actually knew each other, spoke to each other, sat outside in the summer with each other, and told each others' kids not to do certain things —like run away, or cuss—if the kids' parents weren't around, because the values they shared were the same.

At home I had to console myself by dressing up to look like Toby Tyler and pretending that my stuffed monkey was named Mr.

Stubbs, the name of the monkey in the movie who almost steals the show.

But the show belonged to Kevin Corcoran, who had an impish face and came to fame on Walt Disney's television show in the 1950s as Moochie, the little kid on *The Adventures of Spin and Marty*.

He was also in a Disney movie called *Pollyanna,* which starred Haley Mills, with whom I fell in love, as much as a kid under ten can fall in love. She had golden hair and blue eyes, and ever afterward I fell in love with blondes with blue eyes, like Susan in third grade, who snubbed me, and a fourth-grade Susan, who I loved from afar, and so it went until I was 26 and at a friend's birthday party, taking a break with some other friends in the courtyard of the apartment building, and saw the most beautiful blue-eyed blonde I'd ever laid eyes on going upstairs. I told the guys I was with, "I'll see you *later*." Then I ran up the stairs to meet her before anybody else did, and my friend (whose party it was) was giving her a hug, and her back was to me, and my friend saw me and pointed to her, as if to say, "This is the one!" What he meant was that this was the girl he'd been telling me about for years—the most talented and beautiful actress he knew, and the one he'd been trying to get me to meet. But I'd been off in New York acting, and was only here in L.A. because there was an actor's strike going on in the Apple, and I was out here looking for work, and happened to be at the party that night, and therefore decided I had to snag this girl while I had the chance, so I got a dish of peanut M&M's and took her into a corner and started talking with her and when she mentioned going to church the next day I said we might as well go together, and we did, then I took her to brunch—she had an herb omelet, and I knew she was the one. The next date with her was to a movie, a romantic comedy called *Dressed to Kill* directed by Brian de Palma (this is sarcasm, as *Dressed to Kill* was a serial killer movie, and didn't I know how to pick movies to take a date on?)

It must have worked, because two and a half weeks after I met her I asked Cynthia Marie Gagnon to marry me.

She said yes. And that was the best yes of my life, for life does give us yesses and nos, and you learn to enjoy the former and work past the latter, that's the art of living.

Maureen O'Hara died. She was 95. A movie star, known best as John Wayne's tempestuous Irish love in *The Quiet Man*. That's the film where John Wayne physically drags her back to her brother and tosses her on the ground in front of him. "You can have her back!" he says.

The Duke could not get away with that today, even in Ireland.

Another role I liked her in was as the skeptical-of-Santa working mother in *Miracle on 34th Street*. The love interest in that film is played by John Payne, who is really good as the enterprising young lawyer who proves that Kris Kringle is the one and only Santa Claus, at least as far as the state of New York is concerned. Payne changed his image in the 1950s and did some great film noir work, especially in *99 River Street*. There's a saying that came from F. Scott Fitzgerald, to wit, "There are no second acts in American lives," which has to be about the most misguided quote ever to make it into *Bartlett's,* for it is so obviously false. America is the very land of second—and third—acts. John Payne's noir career was his second act, and he killed it. His third act was retirement, which he also killed, having made a bundle of cabbage in the Southern California real estate market.

Maureen O'Hara enjoyed a long career as a screen beauty who could actually act. With her fire-red hair and Irish spirit, she made great foil for stars like Tyrone Power and Errol Flynn, but especially Wayne. Other words that usually describe O'Hara are *spunky* and *spirited*.

Not bad adjectives to go out on.

Meadowlark Lemon died. He was 83. Called "The Clown Prince of Basketball," Lemon played over 16,000 games all over the world with the Harlem Globetrotters, most of those games against the Washington Generals, who were employed to lose every game. What a gig that must have been, being a General. I guess running up and down the court night after night, being the butt of the jokes, but getting paid for it, maybe that wasn't the toughest work in the world. A guy named Red Klotz played for the Generals for most of the glory years, if you want to call them that, and in fact played with them until he was 68 years old, which is a great way to cap off almost seven decades on this round earth, playing round ball.

. . .

Plus Klotz got to watch Lemon and Curly Neal, who could dribble a basketball better than any living being, through his legs, through his ears it seemed like.

Maybe Red Klotz got tired of the same routines, but he never showed it. This was show business as much as basketball, and like a good actor he played his role.

But the star of the show was Lemon, with an infectious smile and joy pouring out of him, joy mainly at making kids laugh and fall in love with the game.

There are other ways to go through life than having joy and a smile that lights up a room, but none better.

Christopher Lee died. He was 93, an actor, and made so many motion pictures that it's difficult to count them all. Some of those movies were real clunkers, like *Police Academy: Mission to Moscow,* but then some of them were immortal, like *Dracula* (the Hammer Films version) and especially *The Lord of the Rings* movies, in which he played Saruman, the perfect foil for Gandalf (Ian McKellen).

Here is the thing that matters: No matter how low budget the film, Christopher Lee always gave it his best shot. That's what a professional does. Even if you're playing Dr. Fu Manchu in a film costing two dollars to make, you do the best Fu Manchu you can do.

At one time in my life I was an actor, and went out on a lot of auditions for commercials. I got several of these. I once handed a tray of hamburgers to someone in a McDonald's commercial. I poured some Pepsi into a glass in a park. I played football on a beach and then knocked back some Colt .45 with the other guys. And in each and every commercial I was Spencer Tracy. I was not there just for the paycheck, although it was nice to get residuals. I was there to be a very serious actor, and no one was going to pour Pepsi like me. I was going to be the Laurence Olivier of Pepsi pourers, the Marlon Brando of soda dispensers.

I suppose Christopher Lee was like that. He and his friend Peter Cushing met on the set of Laurence Olivier's *Hamlet,* where Cushing played Osric and Lee was an extra. They ended up doing Hammer horror films together, and also one of the very best Sherlock Holmes adaptations, Hammer Films' *The Hound of the Baskervilles.* This pair never mailed in their performances.

I've known some performers who've mailed it in. Some authors, too. I was at a book signing once, with several authors at the *Times Festival of Books,* we sat there like ladies of the night winking at sailors, hoping a passerby would come up to us in our appointed hour and buy a book for us to sign. I was sitting next to a bestselling author, who'd been around a long time, had come to the point where anything he wrote would be published and make a dead-certain amount of money for the publisher. He talked

about the ease of his life and how fast he churned out books. I
checked out a couple of his later books and, frankly, they stink.
They are an affront to the readers, who apparently don't care, as
they continue to pay the money.

But Christopher Lee wasn't like that, and I don't ever want to be
like that either.

And now the last entry.

Hannah Rose Winning died. She was 22. Hannah was like a
daughter to me and my wife, as we knew her from the time she
was a baby and met her parents, Charles and Pat, at church. We
watched her grow up. We played and laughed with her. I used to
love to make her laugh. When she was four and her mother said
they were planning a birthday party for her, she asked Hannah
who she'd like to have come. Hannah said "Jeem!" That's how
she pronounced my name, and ever after I was known to the
Winning family as Jeem. It's a name I treasure because Hannah
gave it to me.

Hannah chose to follow Jesus when she was ten years old, and
she did from that day on, with a gentle and generous spirit that
was a wonder to all who knew her.

When Hannah was six, she had to have an operation to correct a
heart valve issue. The surgery was a success, and when she came

out of the anesthetic she reported that while she was under she saw a man in white in the corner of the operating room, watching her, and angels around the doctors and attendants. She made a special point of saying that the angels had noses. Little details that a little girl would remember when actually seeing what was there.

Hannah had to work very hard at her studies, and she did, and eventually got accepted into California Lutheran University. But she had to drop out when she contracted a vicious and rare form of cancer. She had two operations to remove tumors, but they kept coming back, and finally the doctors said there was nothing more they could do.

It was, of course, a stunning blow. Yet somehow Hannah retained her dry sense of humor. One day in the hospital she looked at her father and said, "See? I told you I didn't need to take math." That was Hannah.

She reminded me of the character in C. S. Lewis's *The Chronicles of Narnia*, Reepicheep. He was a little mouse with a sword, and the bravest of Prince Caspian's knights. Hannah was small in stature but her heart and spirit were mountains—majestic, awe-inspiring, life-changing. In her final days she became the greatest example of faith and courage in trauma that I have ever known.

When she was about to leave Cedars Sinai for the last time, she asked to be taken by wheelchair to the hospital chapel. When she got there she said to her father, "Where's the cross?"

. . .

"It's a Jewish hospital," he explained.

Hannah said, "Wheel me to the front." There she bowed her head, lifted her hands and started praying. Her father, mother, sister and close friend all knelt next to her and laid their hands upon her, and quietly wept. Hannah then put her hands on them. "Don't cry," she said. "This is not my body and this is not my home."

And there is no better way to end this book than that.

A NOTE FROM THE AUTHOR

Thank you for reading this book. It was a personal project, a labor of love, a playground for my writer's mind.

If you've found some enjoyment here, please consider writing a review on the book's sales page on Amazon. I would greatly appreciate it!

In the introduction I mentioned William Saroyan, my inspiration for this book. I love writing, but I don't think anybody ever loved writing more than Saroyan. For him, writing was life and life was writing. He would not have survived without it. His personal life was not always the best, but he admitted as much. He once said, "I have made a fiasco of my life, but I have had the right material to work with."

He wrote and wrote, and when his fiction career tailed off due to lack of sales, he turned to memoir and essay and just kept writing. *Obituaries* is the record of a writer fighting off death by writing about it. There's something almost heroic about that.

Well, as I said, I love writing, too, and this book is the result. But I also write thrillers and books about the writing craft, and have been blessed to be able to do that for a living for almost a quarter of a century, and I'm aiming for at least a quarter century more. And which point I will open up renegotiation talks with God, to see if I can squeeze out some more writing time.

Which means I'm going to keep delivering a stream of books and booklets, to entertain and edify, until I can't anymore. Until they find me slumped over the keyboard, my cold dead index finger on the mouse, about to hit *Send*.

If you would like to be among the first to know when I have something new coming out, or offer special deals, then you can join my mailing list (and I don't spam you, or share your address with anyone).

Do that by going to my website: JamesScottBell.com. Then navigate to the FREE BOOK page. Yes, you'll get a free book just for signing up.

You'll also find a list of my other books, thrillers, and books on the writing craft.

Thanks again, friend. And I mean that. Because if you write, if you love to read, and most especially if you do both, you are my friend.

ALSO BY JAMES SCOTT BELL

The Mike Romeo Thriller Series

(in order)

1. Romeo's Rules

2. Romeo's Way

3. Romeo's Hammer

4. Romeo's Fight

5. Romeo's Stand

"Mike Romeo is a terrific hero. He's smart, tough as nails, and fun to hang out with. James Scott Bell is at the top of his game here. There'll be no sleeping till after the story is over." - **John Gilstrap**, New York Times bestselling author of the Jonathan Grave thriller series

The Ty Buchanan Legal Thriller Series

1. Try Dying

2. Try Darkness

3. Try Fear

"Part Michael Connelly and part Raymond Chandler, Bell has an excellent ear for dialogue and makes contemporary L.A. come alive. Deftly plotted, flawlessly executed, and compulsively readable. Bell takes his place among the top authors in the crowded suspense genre." - **Sheldon Siegel**, *New York Times* bestselling author

The Trials of Kit Shannon Historical Legal Thrillers

Book 1 - City of Angels

Book 2 - Angels Flight

Book 3 - Angel of Mercy

Book 4 - A Greater Glory

Book 5 - A Higher Justice

Book 6 - A Certain Truth

"With her shoulders squared and faith set high, Kit Shannon arrives in 1903 Los Angeles feeling a special calling to practice law ... Packed full of genuine, deep and real characters ... The tension and suspense are in overdrive ... A series that is timeless!" — **In the Library Review**

Stand-Alone Thrillers

Your Son Is Alive

Long Lost

Blind Justice

Don't Leave Me

Final Witness

Framed